The Wheelchair Evaluation

The Wheelchair Evaluation:
A Practical Guide

Mitch Batavia, Ph.D., P.T.

Salant Post-Doctoral Fellow, Department of Physical Therapy,
New York University School of Education

Boston   Oxford   Johannesburg   Melbourne   New Delhi   Singapore

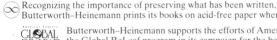

Butterworth–Heinemann supports the efforts of American Forests and the Global ReLeaf program in its campaign for the betterment of trees, forests, and our environment.

Library of Congress Cataloging-in-Publication Data
Batavia, Mitch, 1959-
    The wheelchair evaluation : a practical guide / Mitch Batavia.
        p.   cm.
    Includes bibliographical references and index.
    ISBN 0-7506-7037-1
    1. Wheelchairs--Evaluation.   2. Medical history taking.
3. Orthopedic disability evaluation.   I. Title.
    [DNLM: 1. Wheelchairs. 2. Evaluation Studies. 3. Medical History
    Taking--methods. 4. Body Constitution.   WB 320 B3291w 1998]
    RD757.W4B37 1998
    617'.03--dc21
    DNLM/DLC
    for Library of Congress   98-2710
                                                                       CIP

British Library Cataloguing-in-Publication Data
A catalogue record for this book is available from the British Library.

The publisher offers special discounts on bulk orders of this book.
For information, please contact:

Manager of Special Sales
Butterworth–Heinemann
225 Wildwood Avenue
Woburn, MA 01801-2041
Tel: 781-904-2500
Fax: 781-904-2620

For information on all
Butterworth–Heinemann publications
available, contact our World Wide Web
home page at: http://www.bh.com

10 9 8 7 6 5 4 3 2 1

Printed in the United States of America

*To two individuals who have had a major influence
on my personal and professional growth:
Helmuth Gumprecht and John G. Gianutsos*

Contents

Preface

The purpose of this book is to provide a practical and concise approach for successfully evaluating and recommending a wheelchair for a patient. Although wheelchair evaluation remains a complex and growing area of specialization, little training is provided in professional schools to teach competency in this area. As a result, clinicians learn on the job through trial and error, often with costly mistakes. In a time when third-party payers are cutting back on funding, it is even more critical to conduct competent evaluations and prescribe appropriate, medically justifiable wheelchairs. This manual is a hands-on and concise guide for clinicians and students in health fields who work with physically disabled individuals in need of a wheelchair.

Several unique features of this book distinguish it from other books on wheelchair prescription. First, it is organized to concisely guide the clinician through a logical sequence in the wheelchair prescription process, using a real world (in the trenches) rather than an academic (in the classroom) perspective. The clinician is taken through the necessary steps of patient evaluation, choice of wheelchair components, documentation, and, finally, funding using a letter of medical justification. Second, this book emphasizes history-taking skills, which are missing components in most wheelchair-related books and journal articles. A comprehensive history provides a wealth of vital information that can bear on the success or failure of a wheelchair prescription. Third, this book emphasizes evaluating body shape to successfully fit or match the patient to a wheelchair. Body shape is an area that is not highlighted in the education of the health professional and yet has an important impact on the ultimate fit of an individual with equipment. Fourth, the book was designed to be portable and is therefore small enough for the clinician to carry in the hospital, clinic, school, or nursing home. Finally, this book offers a general approach to patient evaluation with emphasis on breadth rather than depth of subject matter, because it is usually what the clinician forgets to assess that leads to a poor result. A general approach has been used because so many clinical decisions must be made based on unique patient needs, regardless of that patient's diagnosis. A seating system, for example, needs to accommodate a hip extension contracture in a patient regardless of whether that patient has cerebral palsy or a spinal cord injury.

In a similar light, this book focuses on wheelchair features driven by patient need rather than on reviews of specific brand-name components offered by manufacturers, because products may later be added or discontinued. Durable medical equipment dealers and manufacturers can provide information about currently produced, brand-name wheelchair components once the clinician determines the most important features for a patient.

This book provides several unique and practical aids to facilitate wheelchair prescription, including a question-answer format. Critical questions that arise during a wheelchair evaluation are asked and then succinctly addressed.

Algorithms are included to facilitate clinical decision making in choosing wheelchair components. Illustrations are provided to clarify difficult concepts, to educate, and to ease communication between clinicians, family members, patients, durable medical equipment dealers, and manufacturers during a clinic visit. A sample letter of medical justification is included to emphasize information that needs to be communicated to successfully acquire funding for a wheelchair. Exercises included at the end of each chapter can be used to educate a patient and family member in the clinic, the student in the classroom, or as a general review. Every effort has been made to simplify the subject matter in an effort to demystify the wheelchair prescription process and empower health professionals in their clinical decision making. The ultimate goal is to provide better patient care.

The book is organized into four parts and six appendixes. Part I provides a comprehensive overview that the clinician can use to initiate the wheelchair evaluation and prescription process. The overview includes preliminary comments concerning the process, a summary of history taking and physical examination procedures, algorithms for prescribing wheelchair components, and checklists for the wheelchair fitting. A sample evaluation form and a letter of medical justification are included to emphasize important elements of the prescription process. More detailed information on the evaluation and prescription can be found in subsequent chapters.

Part II reviews the patient evaluation. Chapter 2 discusses history taking and includes patient goals, medical problems, lifestyle, social support system, and physical environment. Chapter 3 describes physical examination procedures that are relevant to seating and mobility issues for the wheelchair user. Chapter 4 reviews important functional skills to evaluate for a wheelchair lifestyle.

In Part III, wheelchair components are listed, and advantages and disadvantages of wheelchair frames and seating systems are reviewed. Part IV reviews commonly encountered wheelchair problems and possible causes. Several appendixes treat the ethics involved in wheelchair recommendations, body shape considerations, patient expectations, and skills to teach the caregiver, as well as a directory of durable medical equipment suppliers.

Much of the information in this book was empirically derived while working with children and adults with developmental disabilities, but effort has been made to apply this information to other populations. Information derived from other sources, such as journal articles and texts, are cited to credit, substantiate, or offer a more complete survey of the subject matter. Although solutions to wheelchair problems are suggested throughout the manual, final decisions regarding equipment *must* be made by the health professionals, patient, and family, considering all variables and safety issues specific to each case. Furthermore, the patient's medical status (i.e., fractures, osteoporosis) may prevent the use of some evaluation procedures.

Clinicians may be frustrated by the numerous terms used to refer to the same wheelchair component. An example is *seat belt*, which may also be referred to as *pelvic belt*, *lap belt*, or even *positional belt*. Although attempts are being made to standardize the jargon, variability still exists in the literature and industry. In this book, therefore, effort has been made to include all terms that may refer to a piece of equipment so that the reader can effectively communicate with others who may still be familiar with only one of the terms.

Helping a patient fit well in a wheelchair involves addressing multiple and complex variables that are frequently unique to that individual. As a result, the evaluation process becomes both an art and a science. Much research still needs to be done on the evaluation process to determine how to best serve the patient. An example is the sheer number of variables to consider in choosing a pressure-reducing seat cushion for a patient at risk for pressure sores. Getting it right is not always easy. This book is intended to help health professionals focus on critical areas, anticipate problems, and avoid the "quick-sand" associated with a poor wheelchair prescription. As the wheelchair becomes an extension of the individual and a substitute for the lower limbs, it is imperative that equipment complement the individual's needs and fit together into a functional and harmonious whole.

MB

Acknowledgments

This book came about, in large part, when Mark Cohen at Prentice-Hall (whom I met via the Internet) put me in touch with Barbara Murphy at Butterworth–Heinemann. It was at a meeting with Barbara in San Diego during an American Physical Therapy Association scientific conference that my manuscript finally found a home. To this end, I must thank Mark for his indirect help in setting up this meeting.

I express my appreciation to Butterworth–Heinemann for giving this project life; Barbara Murphy, for believing in this project and sharing my vision; Jana Friedman, for her expertise in seeing the manuscript to completion; and the reviewers for their very helpful comments. I also thank Jane Bangley McQueen, production editor at Silverchair Science + Communications, and Mary Drabot, medical editor at Butterworth–Heinemann, for their efforts to produce a quality product.

I thank Dr. Gabriel Moran of New York University for his guidance and feedback concerning material on ethics.

I thank Suzanne Schry, director of occupational therapy/physical therapy at Terence Cardinal Cooke Health Care Center, for her support in my professional growth and for her vision of improving patient care through seating and positioning. Thanks are also extended to Dr. Howard Adelglass, physiatrist, and Maurice Phillip, orthotics technician, for their assistance in the wheelchair clinic.

I acknowledge Adrienne Bergen, clinician and teacher, for sparking my initial interest in wheelchair evaluations, and wheelchair dealers, such as Jeff Josefson and Paul Amsterdam, for engaging in problem-solving marathons and then spending the extra 2 hours with a patient to see if the "solution" worked.

I wish to express my deepest appreciation to my brother, Professor Andrew I. Batavia, for always encouraging me in my endeavors. (It has meant a lot, Drew.)

Finally, I acknowledge my patients and their families, who have taught me the most.

MB

Introduction and Overview: How to Use This Book

This book is organized into four parts and several appendixes to provide easy access for wheelchair prescription. Part I, Chapter 1 is an overview of the wheelchair prescription process and provides a summary of a suggested sequence for evaluation, important issues in evaluation, algorithms for selecting a wheelchair feature, a sample evaluation form, a sample letter of medical justification for funding, and a checklist for wheelchair fitting. Chapter 1 concludes with a summary of questions for use during the evaluation. For the busy clinician who is familiar with evaluation and prescription, Part I may be sufficient as the primary source during the prescription process. If only a specific wheelchair component needs to be ordered, the clinician can simply refer to a bulleted list and flowchart (algorithm) for that wheelchair component to focus the evaluation and select wheelchair features for that component. The clinician can find additional information on the evaluation process in Parts II–IV in this book.

In Part II, Chapter 2 addresses history taking, Chapter 3 discusses the physical examination (including how to measure a patient for a wheelchair), and Chapter 4 reviews patient skills as they relate to a wheelchair lifestyle. Part III (Chapters 5–7) covers wheelchair selection of mobility bases, postural systems, and wheelchair components and reviews advantages and disadvantages of each item. Part IV (Chapter 8) reviews common wheelchair problems.

Finally, the appendixes discuss related wheelchair issues of body shape, wheelchair myths, ethics of recommending a wheelchair, skills to teach the patient and family, and a directory of wheelchair suppliers.

1

Overview

A successful wheelchair fit requires matching an individual's needs with his or her environment (Table 1.1). Consider the following five areas when evaluating an individual for a wheelchair: (1) patient history, (2) physical impairments, (3) patient skills, (4) the unique body shape of the patient, and (5) the existing wheelchair. These areas provide the clinician with a working hypothesis as to what type of wheelchair may best help the patient. This working hypothesis should then be tested before ordering a wheelchair. The test can come in the form of a trial[1] (borrow the wheelchair) or simulation[2] (putting the patient in a similar physical situation) before the wheelchair is ordered.[3]

Once the wheelchair evaluation is completed and documented, appropriate recommendations concerning the wheelchair need to be made. Frequently, a letter of medical justification is required to secure funding for the patient. This letter includes findings from the evaluation and compelling reasons why the wheelchair is required based on medical necessity.

On approval of the wheelchair, the wheelchair is ordered. Once the wheelchair is delivered, it must be prop-

Table 1.1   Overview of the Wheelchair Evaluation Process

Patient
    Patient history
    Patient physical impairments
    Patient skills
    Unique body shape
Environment
    Existing wheelchair
        Mobility base
        Seating system

Evaluate (patient and environment)
    Hypothesis
        Trial and simulation
            Recommendation and documentation
                Funding
                    Order
                        Fitting
                            Dispensing
                                Follow-up

erly adjusted (the fitting) to the patient. Finally, the patient, family, or both are taught how to safely operate and maintain the wheelchair before it is dispensed. Future follow-up visits may require reinitiation of the wheelchair process to address equipment wear or changing patient needs.

PRELIMINARY COMMENTS

To Clinicians:

- *Designate* one spokesperson for the patient (if more than one advocate comes to clinic).

- *Listen* to the patient, the patient advocate, or both.
    Legitimate requests should be explored.
    Unjustifiable requests require patient or family
        education.
    Use a translator if the language is different from
        yours and effective communication is doubtful.
- *Safety* concerns must be addressed on the day of the
    clinic (e.g., sharp hardware that is cutting into the
    patient should be at least temporarily padded).
- *Teach* proper positioning of the patient and safe use of
    the wheelchair.

Instructions for the Patient and Caregivers

- Bring a list of all problems or issues concerning the
    wheelchair to the clinic. A list ensures that all concerns
    are mentioned on the day of the clinic visit.
- Bring in *all* wheelchair components and related equip-
    ment on the day of the clinic visit (including body jack-
    ets, braces, typical clothing, or any parts that may have
    fallen off the wheelchair).
- Have the patient and caregiver provide information to
    the clinic (e.g., letters, notes, phone numbers) from
    schools, facilities, therapists, or others involved with the
    patient's care.
- Inform the patient and caregiver that wheelchairs
    require medical justification[2] and are therefore based
    on the particular medical needs of the patient.
- Because wheelchairs move and tend to vibrate, parts on
    the wheelchair may loosen with time. The wheelchair

should be periodically checked for loose parts and tightened as necessary. If a part falls off the wheelchair and the family is unsure how to properly attach it, request that the family put the part in a bag or box with the patient's name on it so that the part does not become lost. Then have the family come to the clinic to have the part reattached as soon as possible.

• *Instruct* the patient and caregiver on proper patient positioning in the wheelchair.

Working with Durable Medical Equipment Dealers

New products are released on a yearly basis. It is difficult to keep up with the latest technology and products. That is the dealer's job. Dealers go to trade shows so that they can learn what is new in the world of durable wheelchair equipment to serve clinics better. Clinicians, patients, family, and caregivers should therefore inform the dealer of the problems and needs of the patient.[3] The dealer can then research any new and existing products to address these needs.

Communicating with Durable Medical Equipment Dealers

When the wheelchair recommendation is made, review the order to make sure it is complete and correct. Try to obtain a time frame from the dealer regarding how long it will take to obtain funding and to order the equipment. Things usually take longer than you think, and you will be less frustrated if everyone knows how long it will take ahead of time. Write down the dealer's phone number, so that you can periodically call to determine the status of the wheelchair order. Record dates when paperwork is completed and mailed, so that you know how long to wait before calling to determine the status of an order.

When the wheelchair has been funded, ordered, and delivered, make sure you have what you originally ordered. Also, make sure it is properly fitted to the patient. This is best done at the hospital where the order originated.

If the original evaluation is good, there should be little or no change when the wheelchair is delivered. If everyone is satisfied with the wheelchair, teach the patient and caregiver how to safely operate it, have the patient sign for it, and dispense it. If you are not satisfied, do not have the patient sign for it. Discuss equipment problems with the dealer and reasonable changes in the wheelchair that will make the final fitting acceptable.

Conflicting Patient Goals

Often, there are multiple goals for a patient that conflict when recommending a wheelchair.[1] For example, you may need to maintain the patient in an upright position because of excessive pooling of saliva, yet also need to tilt the patient backward because of forward sliding problems while in the wheelchair. If goals conflict, determine which goals are most important for the patient to achieve. In this particular example, the saliva-pooling issue may take precedence over sliding problems, because pooling of saliva can interfere with patient breathing and lead to aspiration. The sliding problem should then be addressed from an upright sitting position.

SUGGESTED SEQUENCE OF EVALUATION

A suggested sequence is included to minimize the amount of patient handling and lifts (Table 1.2). Take a history, evaluate patient fit and skills, and perform some of the physical examination while the patient sits in the existing wheelchair. Then observe the patient's functional ability in the wheelchair and during transfers to a mat. The dealer can then inspect the condition of the existing wheelchair, while the clinician continues evaluating the patient on the mat. Finally, the patient can return to sitting for evaluation in a new wheelchair or in a simulator.

OVERVIEW OF PATIENT EVALUATION

The patient evaluation consists of the patient's problem, past medical history (including systems review), social history, physical examination, and patient skills. An outline of main areas as they relate to wheelchair prescription is identified to prompt the clinician during the patient evaluation. For further information, the clinician can refer to Chapters 2–4 in Part II of this book.

Table 1.2   Suggested Sequence of the Wheelchair Evaluation

Evaluation	Patient Position
History	Sitting
Evaluate fit in existing wheelchair	Sitting
Physical examination	Sitting
Skills	Sitting and transferring to mat
Physical examination: PROM, anthropometric, skin, and sensation	On mat
Evaluate condition of existing wheelchair	When patient is out of wheelchair
Trial and simulation	Sitting

PROM = passive range of motion.

Chief Complaint

What does the patient say the problem is?

List Problems

List problems in order of importance.

Successes and Failures

Avoid what did not work in previous prescriptions.

Medical History

- *Age*: Children need adjustable components to accommodate future growth.[2]
- *Gender*: Center of gravity and fat distribution differences between men and women can require different postural support requirements.

- *Height*: Tall and short patients may need high and low seat-level heights, respectively.[4,5]
- *Weight*: Heavy patients (e.g., ≥250 lb) may need a heavy-frame construction.
- *Diagnosis*: The type of mobility base and postural support are based in part on the patient's level of physical impairment.
- *Prognosis*[1,6]: Prognosis may determine whether a wheelchair is rented or purchased.
- *Precautions*[6]: Are there weightbearing, range of motion (ROM), or exertion restrictions?
- *Surgeries*: Orthopedic surgeries can alter anthropometrics and postural needs.
- *Physical rehabilitation*: Gains in therapy can reduce equipment needs.
- *Medication*[7]: Drowsiness due to medications can make power mobility unsafe.
- *Orthotics*: Additional space in wheelchair may be required.
- *Systems review*: For thoroughness, do a chart review of major organ systems.

Social History

- *Residence*: Determine wheelchair accessibility[8] (32-in. clearance recommended for doorways; 36 in. for corridors).
- *Caregivers*: Is support available to maintain equipment (e.g., power mobility, batteries)?

- *Indoor and outdoor use*: Consider durable frames, shock absorption features, and appropriate power mobility needs for outdoor and rough-terrain use.
- *Table-surface requirements for work, school, and eating*: Determine appropriate armrest style (e.g., desk-type armrests for access to tables, full-length armrests for upper extremity [UE] activities using a lap board).
- *Travel*: Consider lightweight folding wheelchair for car transportation and storage; tie-down feature for bus travel.
- *Hours sitting*: Extended periods of time sitting (i.e., up time) can require a pressure cushion with greater pressure-reduction properties.
- *Age of existing wheelchair*: Equipment age may determine warranty period, suggests amount of wear, and clues the clinician as to when patient was last funded.

Physical Examination

- *Passive ROM*: Determine if patient has sufficient lower extremity (LE) ROM (i.e., 90-degree hip flexion) to fit into a standard wheelchair[3] and UE ROM to reach handrims.
- *Anthropometric measurements*: Measure the patient's seat depth, seat width, back height, and heel-to-knee distances to determine frame size.[9]
- *Skin*: Determine risk for pressure-sore development and need for a pressure-reducing cushion, gravity-assisted positioning, or both to redistribute pressure between patient's buttocks and seat surface.

- *Sensation*: If patient is insensate, a pressure-reducing cushion may be needed. If vision is diminished, power mobility may be unsafe.
- *Postural alignment*: If significant fixed asymmetric deformities of the trunk or pelvis are present, custom-molded postural inserts may be required.[3, 10]
- *Active movement*: If no movement or weight-shifting ability is possible, consider a good pressure-reducing cushion. If patient self-propels, consider a manual wheelchair. If not, consider a power wheelchair using control switches. Pad wheelchair if activity-related injuries are possible.
- *Sitting balance*: Consider lateral and anterior trunk supports if balance is poor. Use reclining or backward tilt-in-space wheelchair to decrease reliance on anterior trunk supports.
- *Primitive reflexes*: Block movements that trigger undesirable reflex activity.
- *Tone*: Low tone may require reclining or backward tilt-in-space wheelchairs to discourage trunk collapse. Spasticity may require foot straps to maintain feet on footrests. Extensor tone requires adequate pelvic stabilization.
- *Endurance*: A lighter weight, manual wheelchair or power mobility may be needed for patients with limited endurance.
- *Strength*: Improve propulsion efficiency if needed (e.g., lightweight frame and wheels; coated, large handrims; camber rear wheels; optimize position of patient relative to rear axis using multiple adjustable axis).

- *Memory*: Memory is required to perform wheelchair procedures (e.g., transfers) safely.
- *Cognition*[11]: Means-end (intentional) behavior required to operate power mobility.
- *Perception and judgment*[12]: Consider the issue of safe power mobility.

Patient Skills

- *Locomotion*: Unsafe or nonfunctional ambulation requires self-propulsion of a manual wheelchair. Non-functional self-propulsion requires safe power mobility or an attendant-operated wheelchair.
- *Transfers*: Evaluate appropriate seat cushion (e.g., stability), front rigging (e.g., swing-away, detachable features), and armrests (e.g., adjustable, removable features) to facilitate specific transfer requirements.
- *Sitting*: A high back support may be needed for patients with inadequate spinal support, decreased trunk control, and lower activity level in wheelchair.[13]
- *UE function*: Evaluate ability to self-propel or operate power mobility switches and controls.

OVERVIEW OF WHEELCHAIR SELECTION ALGORITHMS

Selection of a wheelchair requires choosing the most appropriate features based on the patient's needs. The following information can assist the busy clinician in prescribing wheelchairs. Bulleted lists and algorithms in this chapter can help the clinician focus on patient evaluation areas and choose appropriate wheelchair components. For more in-depth information on wheelchair components, refer to Chapters 6 and 7.

Mobility bases are organized by the patient's propulsion ability and postural needs. Wheelchair components include rear wheels and tires, casters, armrests, front rigging, footrests, handrims, and wheel locks (Figure 1.1). Postural supports include seat cushions, seat inserts, back inserts, anterior and lateral trunk supports, head supports, lap boards, positioning blocks, straps, and seat belts.

It may be possible to order more than one feature for a particular wheelchair component. For example, an armrest may be adjustable in height, removable, and double length. On the other hand, not all manufacturers offer the same features.

The key is to evaluate what the patient needs and then ask the dealer or manufacturer if the component with the needed features can be provided. A list of manufacturers with telephone numbers is provided in Appendix 6.

Mobility Base

The mobility base or frame provides the structure and mobility for the wheelchair. It may be useful to think of types of mobility bases by propulsion ability and body positioning of the patient. Your evaluation needs to be fairly comprehensive to determine a mobility base.

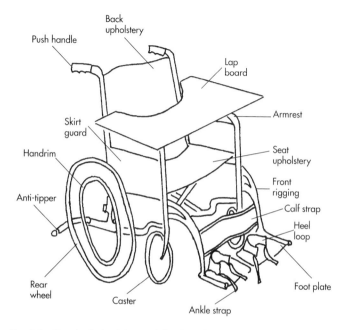

Fig. 1.1 Standard wheelchair with lap board.

Focus of Evaluation for Mobility Bases

- ROM of LEs to fit in standard frame
- UE or LE function for wheelchair propulsion
- Posterior stability in wheelchair
- Sitting ability

- Cognition, judgment, and medication for safe power mobility
- Muscle tone
- Ability to operate a control switch
- Type of transfer
- Activity level
- Indoor or outdoor use

Type of Mobility Base (Based on Propulsion Ability)

Determine if the patient is capable of self-propelling a manual wheelchair and how this will be accomplished (i.e., both arms, one arm, feet). If self-propulsion is not feasible, determine if safe power mobility is possible. If only attendant-operated propulsion is possible, determine if the wheelchair will be used solely indoors or indoors and outdoors (Figure 1.2). Possible mobility bases that address propulsion needs for different patient populations include standard,[6] amputee,[5] ultralight,[14] one-hand drive,[4] hemiplegic,[4] indoor,[4] geriatric chairs,[5] power mobility,[15] scooters,[4] and strollers.

Type of Mobility Base (Based on Patient Orientation)

For mobility bases that change patient orientation, determine if the patient is capable of sitting in an upright position, whether gravity-assisted recline or tilt is required due to poor sitting ability, or if a standing orientation is needed for the patient's vocation and avocation (Figure 1.3). Possible choices of mobility bases to address patient orientation include standard,[6] reclining,[9] tilt-in-space,[16] and standing frames.[17]

How does patient propel?

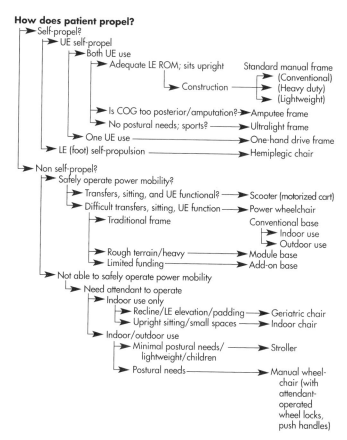

Fig. 1.2 Mobility base algorithm based on propulsion ability. (UE = upper extremity; LE = lower extremity; ROM = range of motion; COG = center of gravity.)

How will patient be oriented in wheelchair?

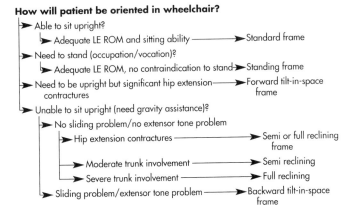

Fig. 1.3 Mobility base algorithm based on orientation need. (LE = lower extremity; ROM = range of motion.)

Seat Belts and Pelvic Positioning Devices

Seat belts provide safety during transportation. They can also be used as positioning belts to help stabilize the patient's pelvis to maintain good postural alignment. Focus your evaluation on hand function, posture, muscle tone, and body size. Determine the patient's ability to operate different types of seat belts. The choices of seat belts include hook and loop, buckle with movable tongue, airplane, auto, and molded clips. Evaluate the need for additional pelvic stabilization by using peroneal straps[18] or a sub anterior superior iliac spine bar[5] to address strong extensor tone or sliding problems (Figure 1.4). Choose belt size based on body size (Figure 1.5).

What type of seat belt?

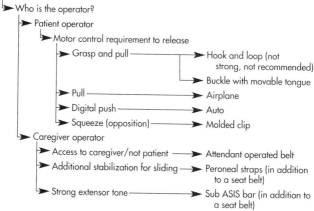

Fig. 1.4 Seat belt and pelvic positioning device algorithm. (ASIS = anterior superior iliac spine.)

Focus of Evaluation for Seat Belts and Positioning Belts

- Hand function to operate belt
- Anthropometrics (body size) to determine belt length and width
- Postural support needs at pelvis
- Amount of extensor tone

Front Rigging

Front rigging provides a support surface for the patient's lower legs and feet. Focus the evaluation on

What seat belt size?

Small children[18] —————→ 1-in.–wide belt
Large children[18] —————→ 1½-in.–wide belt
Adult[18] —————→ 2-in.–wide belt
Heavy adult —————→ Extra length

Fig. 1.5 Size of seat belt algorithm.

LE ROM, transfer abilities, and tolerance for dependent LEs. Choice of features[14, 19] include fixed front rigging with flip-up foot plates and swing-away, detachable, and elevating front rigging (Figure 1.6). The patient with double above-knee (AK) amputations obviously does not need front rigging, and patients who use their feet to propel may only need front rigging for support during long-distance transportation.

Focus of Evaluation for Front Rigging

- Knee ROM limitations (e.g., ankylosis of knee)
- Cast (LE)
- Type of transfer
- Edema, poor tolerance for dependent position
- Environment (e.g., small living spaces)
- Diagnosis (e.g., AK amputation)
- Self-propulsion using LE

Foot Plates

Foot plates provide a flat support surface for the feet. Determine type of foot plate based on need to support

What type of front rigging based on knee position?

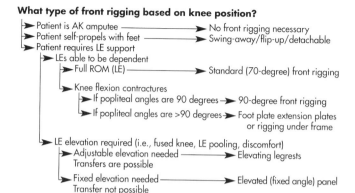

- Patient is AK amputee ⟶ No front rigging necessary
- Patient self-propels with feet ⟶ Swing-away/flip-up/detachable
- Patient requires LE support
  - LEs able to be dependent
    - Full ROM (LE) ⟶ Standard (70-degree) front rigging
    - Knee flexion contractures
      - If popliteal angles are 90 degrees ⟶ 90-degree front rigging
      - If popliteal angles are >90 degrees ⟶ Foot plate extension plates or rigging under frame
  - LE elevation required (i.e., fused knee, LE pooling, discomfort)
    - Adjustable elevation needed ⟶ Elevating legrests
      Transfers are possible
    - Fixed elevation needed ⟶ Elevated (fixed angle) panel
      Transfer not possible

What type of front rigging based on transfers/maneuverability features?

- Lightweight ⟶ Flip-up front rigging
- Access to small spaces ⟶ Swing-away front rigging
- Maneuver within small spaces ⟶ Detachable front rigging

Fig. 1.6 Front rigging algorithm. (AK = above-knee; LE = lower extremity; ROM = range of motion.)

the patient's feet in whatever available ankle range, foot range, and foot location is possible. Focus the evaluation on LE ROM, body dimensions, and postural symmetry of the LEs. Foot plate features include standard, adjustable angle, foot-plate extenders, one-piece foot boards, and a custom foot box (Figure 1.7). Consider a larger size foot plate to support large feet and to protect toes if they over-hang or if there is the possibility of trauma from bumping into walls.

What kind of foot plate support?

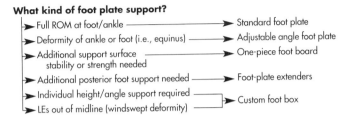

Fig. 1.7   Foot plate algorithm. (ROM = range of motion; LE = lower extremity.)

Focus of Evaluation for Foot Plates

- ROM limitations: foot and ankle deformity
- Anthropometrics: leg length discrepancy, foot size
- Posture: LEs windswept

Rear Wheels

Rear wheels permit the wheelchair to roll. Rear-wheel selection is based on several features, such as wheel weight versus durability,[20] angle of the wheels, storage, and adjustability of rear-wheel position on the frame. As previously noted in Overview of Wheelchair Selection Algorithms, it is possible to request more than one feature for your patient. For example, your patient may need spokeless (molded) wheels that are cambered and have a quick-release feature to address durability, lateral stability, and portability requirements (Figure 1.8).

What rear wheel features?

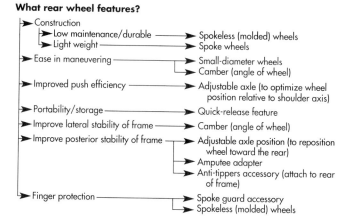

Fig. 1.8 Rear wheel algorithm.

Focus of Evaluation for Rear Wheels

- Need for propulsion efficiency and maneuverability
- Need for stability
- Need for storage
- Need for durability
- Need for lightweight wheelchair

Rear Tires

Rear tires surround the rear wheels, contact the ground, and transmit forces to and from the wheelchair. Focus the evaluation on whether the wheelchair is to be

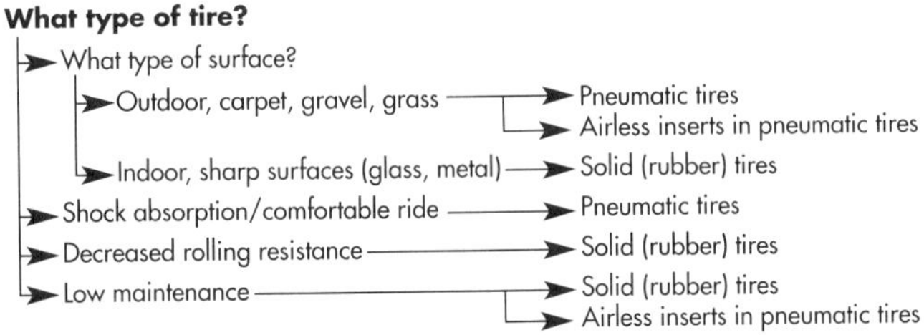

What type of tire?

Fig. 1.9 Tire algorithm.

used primarily indoors or outdoors. Three types of tires include solid,[4] pneumatic (air),[1] and airless (solid insert) (Figure 1.9). If a pneumatic (air-filled) tire is selected, consider ordering an air pump to maintain proper tire-pressure level.

Focus of Evaluation for Rear Tires

- Indoor or outdoor terrain
- Ability to maintain equipment
- Comfortable ride
- Rolling resistance of tire

Handrims

Handrims are mounted on the rear wheels and are grasped by the patient to self-propel the wheelchair. Evaluate handrim diameter according to speed or strength requirements of the patient during self-

Size of handrim?

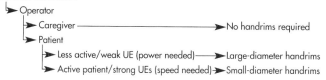

Should handrims be covered?

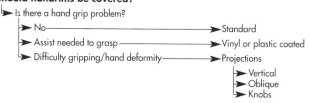

Fig. 1.10 Handrim algorithm. (UE = upper extremity.)

propulsion. Determine need for coated rims or projections based on patient's hand function. Choice of handrims include different size diameters[14, 20] and whether rims are standard (uncoated), coated,[14] or have projections[20] (Figure 1.10). Consider the use of gloves to reduce the risk of friction burns from handrims when stopping the wheelchair.

Focus of Evaluation for Handrims

- Hand function and deformity
- Strength of UEs
- Speed requirements (e.g., for sports)

What size casters?

- Comfortable ride/shock absorption → Large casters; pneumatic (air) tires
- Rolling over obstacles → Large casters
- Maneuverability/sports/minimal flutter → Small casters
- Clearance needed for front rigging → Small casters
- Use on sand → Ball (wide) caster

Fig. 1.11 Caster algorithm.

Casters

Casters[19] are small wheels (usually in the front) that enable the wheelchair to turn and change direction. Determine caster size according to caster performance requirements (e.g., shock absorption, maneuverability, negotiation over cracks). Choice of caster sizes range in diameter from 2 in. to 8 in. (Figure 1.11). Tires may be pneumatic, semipneumatic, or solid (rubber).

Focus of Evaluation for Casters

- Need for comfortable ride
- Need for maneuverability and performance
- Surface conditions
- Clearance of front rigging

Wheel Locks (Brakes)

Wheel locks[4] prevent the wheelchair from rolling. Evaluate the patient's motor ability to independently operate wheel locks. Wheel locks can be toggle or level in style and

Type of wheel locks?

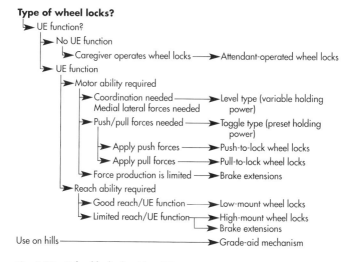

Fig. 1.12   Wheel lock algorithm. (UE = upper extremity.)

can be mounted high or low depending on the patient's level of function and ability to reach (Figure 1.12).

Focus of Evaluation for Wheel Locks

- UE coordination, strength, and reach
- Hilly terrain

Armrests

Armrests[14, 19] provide support for the UE. Determine the type of armrest based on type of transfers; UE support

What are functional requirements for the armrest?

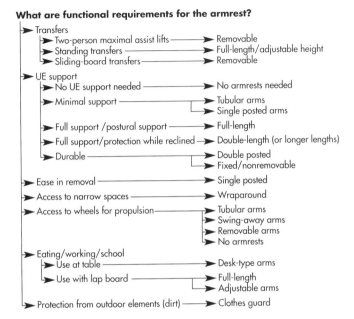

Fig. 1.13 Armrest algorithm. (UE = upper extremity.)

needs; and requirements for work, school, and eating. Armrest features address armrest length, height adjustability, detachability, durability, and impact on overall wheelchair width (Figure 1.13).

Focus of Evaluation for Armrests

- Type of transfers
- Amount of UE support needed
- School and work: use of desk or lap board
- Clearance for doorways
- Ability to reach wheels to self-propel
- Use of reclining frame

Lap Boards

Lap boards[4, 6, 17, 21] rest over the armrests and provide a table surface for the patient while he or she is in the wheelchair. Determine if the patient needs a lap board for additional UE support and rest, feeding, programming activities, communication, or power-control interfacing. Lap board features include the option of solid or clear materials, cut-out areas for clearance to reach rear wheels or for joystick placement, easels and overlays for communication, rims to prevent objects from falling from the edge of the board, and straps to keep the board from sliding off the wheelchair (Figure 1.14).

Consider the type of hardware used to secure the lap board to the armrest, because some mechanisms are more difficult to operate and less reliable in performance than others. Note that lap boards generally require the support of full-length armrests and may tip forward if secured to desk-type armrests.

Lap board requirements

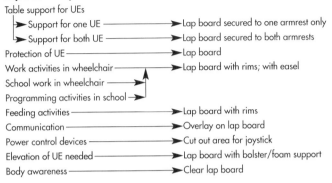

Fig. 1.14   Lap board algorithm. (UE = upper extremity.)

Focus of Evaluation for Lap Boards

- UE edema requiring elevation
- Painful shoulder requiring support
- Table surface for work, school, and play activities
- Surface for communication or feeding
- Perceptual neglect of a UE

Seat Inserts

Seat inserts[22] provide postural support for the pelvis, hips, and LE (thighs). Evaluate the amount of postural support needed to prevent a hammock effect (i.e., LE adduction and internal rotation caused by a sling type seat) on the patient's hips. Determine the amount of contoured shap-

How much postural deformity is there?

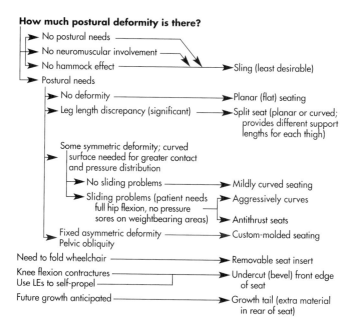

Fig. 1.15   Seat insert algorithm. (LE = lower extremity.)

ing of the seat needed to accommodate deformity and redistribute pressure areas. Seat inserts can be planar, curved, or custom molded (Figure 1.15).

Focus of Evaluation for Seat Inserts

- Degree of deformity and need to redistribute pressure
- Leg length discrepancy

- Sliding problems
- Sensation
- Skin integrity and risk factors for pressure sores
- Cushion to be used with seat insert

Seat Cushions

Seat cushions[20, 22, 23] provide comfort and pressure reduction. *No perfect cushion exists for all patients.* Evaluate cushion features (e.g., stabile, easy cleaning, lightweight, pressure reduction, comfort) that are important for your patient. Note that a protective (incontinent) cover is needed to protect foam cushions that absorb moisture (i.e., open-cell foams). Order two covers, so that one can be laundered while the other is in use. Static seat cushions use foam, air, gel, or a combination of these materials. Dynamic seats, on the other hand, use a power source to reduce sitting pressure (Figure 1.16).

Focus of Evaluation for Seat Cushions

- Incontinence (ease in cleaning cushion)
- Weight considerations of cushion
- Caregiver level of support to maintain and monitor cushion condition
- Stability for sitting and transfers
- Skin integrity, sensation, and mobility
- Pressure-reducing characteristics of cushion (evaluated individually for each patient)
- Risk factors for pressure sores

What are seat cushion requirements?

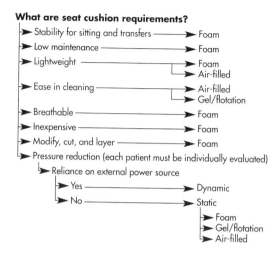

Fig. 1.16 Seat cushion algorithm.

Back Inserts

Back inserts[3] provide postural support for the patient's trunk and spine. Evaluate the amount of postural support needed to prevent a hammock effect (i.e., rounding of the spine due to a sling-type back support) on the trunk and the amount of contoured back support needed to accommodate a fixed spinal deformity. Determine height requirements of back insert by assessing the patient's sitting balance and self-propulsion activity level. Back inserts, like seat inserts, can be planar, curved (contoured), or custom molded (Figure 1.17).

How much postural support or spinal deformity is present?

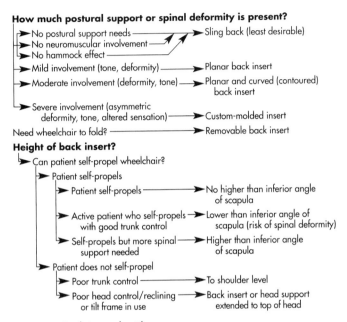

Fig. 1.17   Back insert algorithm.

Focus of Evaluation for Back Inserts

- Degree of spinal deformity and need to redistribute pressure
- Sitting balance
- Activity level (e.g., sports)
- Tone
- Sensation

Trunk Supports

Trunk supports[3,5] encourage midline posture and discourage anterior or lateral listing of the trunk. Evaluate if sitting balance or spinal alignment is insufficient anteriorly or laterally. If a harness is considered, assess safety concerns related to straps near the neck area (i.e., risk of strangulation), patient tolerance of straps, and facility policy on restraints. Trunk supports, which include lateral trunk supports, chest straps, chest harnesses (several styles), shoulder retractors, and shoulder straps (indirect trunk supports), and use of gravity (Figure 1.18) should be recommended and used as positioning devices rather than as restraints. Try to use the least restrictive and safest approach to achieve seating goals.

Focus of Evaluation for Trunk Supports

- Postural and spinal alignment
- Sitting balance
- Tone and reflexes
- Tactile defensiveness and sensitivity
- Facility policy on restraints

Headrest and Supports

Headrests[3,4,16,18] provide midline support for the patient's head if required. Evaluate the patient's ability to maintain midline position of the head. (Make sure head position is not due to inadequate trunk support.) Inspect the shape of the head posteriorly for an occipital ridge area. Deter-

How is trunk control?

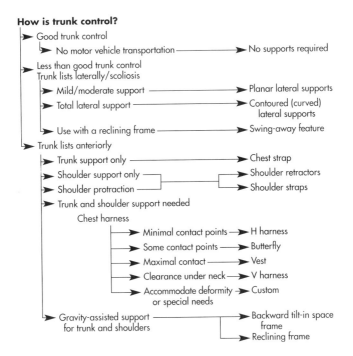

Fig. 1.18   Trunk support algorithm.

mine if the patient needs head support while traveling by public transportation in a wheelchair. Assess safety issues and ability of caregivers to adequately monitor patients who use equipment around the neck or head (i.e., neck rings, head bands). Head supports can incorporate planar or curved shapes, side panels and pads, neck collars, head rings, and the use of gravity assistance (Figure 1.19).

Focus of Evaluation for Headrest and Supports

- Head control
- Sitting balance
- Tone and reflexes
- Shape of the head (anthropometrics)
- Use of motor vehicle transportation in wheelchair
- Proper supervision available
- Forward sliding activity

Positioning Blocks and Straps

Positioning blocks and straps can help some patients maintain a more neutral and midline position while in the wheelchair. Determine if the patient's extremities are in or out of midline. Positioning blocks include protraction blocks, hip guides, knee adductors, pommels, and knee blocks. Straps and webbing include heel loops and ankle straps (Figure 1.20).

Focus of Evaluation for Positioning Blocks and Straps

- Asymmetric postural alignment of UEs and LEs
- Muscle tone and pathologic reflexes

How good is head control?

- Good head control
  - No motor vehicle transportation ⟶ No headrest required
  - Motor vehicle transportation in wheelchair ⟶ Consider removable headrest

- Head control is not good
  - Head lists backward
    Reclining frame in use
    - No neck hyperextension ⟶ Planar posterior headrest
    - Neck hyperextends ⟶ Planar posterior headrest with occipital ridge (if occipital ridge is tolerated)
  - Head lists backward and laterally
    - Mild support/centering needed ⟶ Mildly curved headrest (occipital ridge if tolerated)
    - Aggressive support needed (head hooking) ⟶ Moderately (deep/wide) curved headrests (occipital ridge if tolerated)
      ⟶ Central and side panels (occipital ridge if tolerated)
      ⟶ Neck ring (if safe and adequate supervision is available)
  - Head lists forward
    - Client can sit reclined or tilted?
      - Gravity-assisted support ⟶ Backward tilt-in space frame/ reclining frame
    - If client must sit upright? ⟶ Head band and other anterior head supports (if safe and adequate supervision is available)

Fig. 1.19   Head support algorithm.

Positioning block or strap requirements

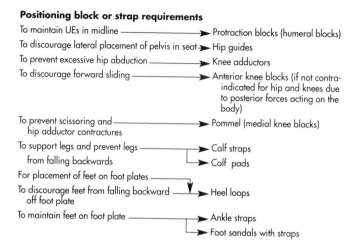

To maintain UEs in midline ⟶ Protraction blocks (humeral blocks)

To discourage lateral placement of pelvis in seat ⟶ Hip guides

To prevent excessive hip abduction ⟶ Knee adductors

To discourage forward sliding ⟶ Anterior knee blocks (if not contra-indicated for hip and knees due to posterior forces acting on the body)

To prevent scissoring and hip adductor contractures ⟶ Pommel (medial knee blocks)

To support legs and prevent legs from falling backwards ⟶ Calf straps / Calf pads

For placement of feet on foot plates ⟶
To discourage feet from falling backward off foot plate ⟶ Heel loops

To maintain feet on foot plate ⟶ Ankle straps / Foot sandals with straps

Fig. 1.20   Positioning blocks and straps algorithm. (UE = upper extremity.)

Storage

Finally, think of storage needs for your patient, such as utility bags for medication, storage racks for assistive devices and feeding poles, and of course the storability of the wheelchair itself (Figure 1.21).

SAMPLE WHEELCHAIR EVALUATION FORM

A sample wheelchair evaluation form is included, although clinicians may prefer to use their own form, use additional pages, or describe an evaluation in paragraph

Things to store or support

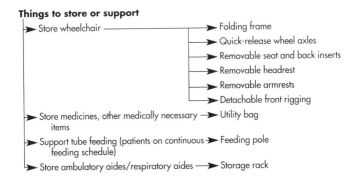

Fig. 1.21 Storage algorithm.

form (Form 1.1). Note that the evaluation form follows the sequence of the patient evaluation and documents critical information required for the wheelchair prescription. Also note that this form emphasizes the medical justification of *every* wheelchair component, which is important when funding is requested.

SAMPLE LETTER OF MEDICAL JUSTIFICATION FOR A NEW WHEELCHAIR

A sample letter of medical justification is included to highlight important issues that should be documented when requesting funding for a wheelchair (Form 1.2). The letter incorporates all relevant information derived from the evaluation yet is written to tell a story. The letter

Name _____ Date _____ DOB _____

Insurance No. _____ Chart No. _____

Funding _____ Contacts _____

Chief complaint _____

List problems _____

Successes and failures _____

Past Medical History

Age _____ Gender _____ Height _____ Weight _____

Diagnosis _____ Prognosis _____

Surgeries _____

Physical rehabilitation _____ Medication _____

Orthotics _____

Systems Review _____

Physical Examination

Passive range of motion _____

Anthropometric measurements _____

Skin _____ Sensation _____

Postural alignment _____ Active movement _____

Sitting balance _____ Primitive reflexes _____

Tone _____ Endurance _____ Strength _____ Cognition _____

Perception _____ Judgment _____

Patient Skills

Locomotion _____ Transfers _____ Sitting _____

Upper extremity function _____

Form 1.1 Wheelchair evaluation and recommendation form.

Social History

Residence _____ Level of support _____

Indoor and outdoor use _____

Table requirements _____ Travel requirements _____

Hours sitting _____ Age of existing wheelchair _____

Wheelchair Recommendation	**(What) Component**	**(Why) Medical Justification**

Mobility base

    Frame size _____

    Armrests _____

    Front rigging _____

    Wheel locks _____

    Rear wheels and tires _____

    Handrims _____

    Casters and tires _____

Postural support system

    Seat cushions _____

    Seat insert _____

    Back insert _____

    Trunk support _____

    Head support _____

    Seat belt and pelvic

       stabilization _____

    Straps and positioning blocks _____

    Lap board _____

Accessories _____

Form 1.1   *continued*

The Clinic
XYZ Avenue
New York, NY 33333
Phone: (212) 123-4567

To: Funding agency
Re: Jane Smith: Letter of medical justification for a new wheelchair
Chart #: 98765
DOB: 4/27/70
Funding No.:   # SN0000N

January 1, 1999

To Whom It May Concern:

 Jane Smith is a 16-year-old female with a diagnosis of cerebral palsy.
Functional Status
 Functionally, Jane Smith is nonambulatory, dependent in all activities of
daily living, and requires total support to sit and transfer (two-person lifts).
She has no functional use of her upper extremities, does not self-propel her
wheelchair, and cannot operate power mobility. Jane Smith therefore relies
on caregivers to transport her. She uses her wheelchair for both postural
support and transportation to the clinic, school, and park.
Clinical Status
 Clinically, Jane Smith's lower extremity range of motion is within functional limits for sitting. Hip flexion is 90 degrees, hip abduction is full, hip
rotation is neutral, popliteal angles are 60 degrees bilaterally, and ankle
range is within functional limits distally. Jane Smith is motorically inactive,
and muscle tone is low. Posturally, she presents with a forward head, flexible
kyphotic trunk, and a posterior pelvic tilt. Trunk and head control are poor,
and she tends to list her trunk forward while in an upright sitting position.
Skin is intact although pressure (redness) is noted over her greater trochanters
and additional redness is noted under the client's ischia, which is lacking in
soft tissue protection. In terms of anthropometrics, hip-to-hip seat-width measures 16 in., and she has a 1.5-in. leg length discrepancy (left side is shorter).
Existing Wheelchair
 Jane Smith's existing standard wheelchair (16 in. wide × 16 in. deep),
is 4 years old and no longer provides adequate (1) width, (2) postural
support, or (3) pressure relief for this client.

Form 1.2 Sample letter of medical justification for a new wheelchair.

1. *The existing wheelchair is too narrow.* Her mother reports significant weight gain (20 lb) and growth (5 in.) since Jane received her wheelchair 4 years ago. She is using a wheelchair with a 16-in. seat width, which is too narrow for her hip-to-hip seat width, which currently measures 16 in. Remaining in the existing narrow wheelchair may lead to ulcer development due to excessive pressure of her greater trochanters against the inside panels of the armrests. She therefore needs a wider wheelchair frame (18 in.) that can accommodate her seat width, clothing, and any future growth.

2. *The existing wheelchair no longer provides sufficient postural support.* Jane Smith has poor sitting and can no longer tolerate upright sitting in her standard wheelchair frame. Her school teacher reports that Jane has difficulty participating in class activities because of her sitting difficulties. Poor sitting balance, poor head control, and low muscle tone contribute to her forward head, collapsing (kyphotic) trunk, tendency to list her trunk anteriorly, and forward sliding of her pelvis while in the wheelchair. The use of a chest harness has been poorly tolerated and its use has become a safety concern because of the patient's tendency to slide forward and having her neck become caught in the chest harness. Unfortunately, her existing standard frame cannot tilt backwards to provide the gravity-assisted postural support she needs. Jane Smith needs a backward tilt-in-space frame that will provide gravity-assisted postural support and minimize reliance on anterior trunk supports.

3. *The existing foam cushion is completely worn* (i.e., "bottomed out") *and no longer provides comfort or pressure reduction.* As a result, she is beginning to show signs of skin tissue compromise at the ischia and cries if she sits longer than 20 minutes.

Evaluation of New Wheelchair

Jane Smith was evaluated in a wider (18 in. wide × 16 in. deep), backward tilt-in-space wheelchair frame with a gel cushion on 12/15/98. She tolerated the backward tilt (25 degrees) with good head and trunk alignment, no anterior listing of the trunk, and no forward pelvic sliding for functional durations of 90 minutes. (See enclosed photographs.) Her mother reported that she was more comfortable (i.e., she fell asleep during part of the evaluation), and her school teacher reported that it was easier for Jane to participate in class-type activities while positioned in better alignment. At the conclusion of the evaluation, no erythema (i.e., redness) was noted at her hips or ischia.

Form 1.2 *continued*

Wheelchair Recommendations

A new wheelchair with a backward tilt-in-space frame is recommended to accommodate Jane Smith's body dimension and postural alignment needs. These problems can no longer be addressed with her existing standard wheelchair.

Mobility Base

A (Brand X) backward tilt-in-space wheelchair will provide gravity-assisted postural support.

- *Size*: Adult size (18 in. wide × 16 in. deep) to accommodate clothing, body width, and future growth.
- *Front rigging*: Standard 70-degree front rigging secondary to full range of motion.
- *Armrests*: Adjustable height; removable; full-length armrests to support a lap board, provide an appropriate upper extremity support level, and facilitate two-person transfer activities.
- *Wheel locks*: Attendant-operated locks for operation by the caregiver. Wheel locks are necessary for safety during transfer activities.
- *Rear wheels*: 24-in. diameter spokeless wheels with pneumatic tires for shock absorption and comfortable ride outdoors, to school, and to the park.
- *Casters*: Large, 8-in. diameter casters with semipneumatic tires for low-maintenance care. Large casters will facilitate negotiation over cracks and objects outdoors.
- *Handrims*: Not required because client cannot self-propel.

Postural Support System

- *Seat insert*: Split seat insert with mild curve to accommodate a 1.5-in. leg length discrepancy and provide more contact points to distribute pressure under the client's buttocks.
- *Seat cushion*: (Brand X) gel cushion. Gel material is easy to clean, may act to simulate fat tissue, and was tolerated well during the evaluation. (Pressure areas were previously noted with existing foam cushion.) Pressure reduction in this client is necessary due to risk of pressure-sore development (reduced soft tissue around ischia, low motor activity, incontinence, history of pressure-related redness).
- *Cushion covers*: Two incontinence covers to facilitate cleaning and protect cushion from feces and urine due to client incontinence.
- *Back insert*: Planar-shaped back insert, up to shoulder height, to provide necessary spinal support due to poor sitting balance.

Form 1.2   *continued*

- *Trunk supports*:
    - *Curved lateral trunk supports* to discourage lateral trunk listing due to poor trunk control and to promote vertical alignment of the trunk in the coronal plane. Curved supports provide greater points of contact for this low-tone client.
    - *Chest strap* to discourage anterior trunk listing.
- *Head support*: Curved headrest with an occipital ridge to address poor head control and encourage midline position of client's head. An occipital ridge can help discourage hyperextension of the client's head.
- *Seat belt*: Auto seat belt with a 2-in. width, positioned at a 45-degree angle to maintain proper pelvic positioning, prevent forward sliding of the pelvis, and for safety during transportation.
- *Ankle straps*: Hook and loop fastener straps to maintain feet on foot plates.
- *Heel loops*: To maintain proper placement of feet on foot plates and prevent feet from falling posteriorly from footrests.
- *Lap board*: For upper extremity support, for programming activities at school, and for support while eating at school and home.
- *Protraction blocks*: Attached to the lap board to prevent the client's upper extremities from falling behind the board while the wheelchair is in a backward tilt position.

Accessories
- *Air pump*: To maintain sufficient air pressure in pneumatic tires.

In summary, an 18-in., backward tilt-in-space wheelchair system with a gel cushion is medically necessary to discourage postural deformity and prevent the incidence of pressure-sore development at the ischia and greater trochanters in this client. The wheelchair will also improve her comfort level and enable her to participate more fully in school.

Thank you for your attention regarding Jane Smith and her need for a new wheelchair. Please contact us if you need additional information about this request.

Sincerely yours,
Mitchell Batavia, Ph.D., P.T.
John Doe, M.D.

Form 1.2   *continued*

should describe the patient's condition, wheelchair-related problems, how these problems impact the patient's condition, and how a new prescription would remedy the patient's medically related problem. Above all, the letter must *medically justify* this new prescription.

The first three paragraphs in the sample letter include patient diagnoses (also past medical history), functional status, clinical status, and social history, as they pertain to the patient's wheelchair needs. In the next paragraph, the letter focuses on problems with the existing wheelchair. In the fifth paragraph, evaluation of the patient for the new wheelchair is documented with an objective report of the outcome. Finally, the new wheelchair is recommended with justification of every wheelchair component and postural support. (If custom components are ordered, justification should be provided as to why less costly, commercially available components would not be medically appropriate for this patient.) The closing paragraph re-emphasizes why the wheelchair recommended is medically necessary for the patient.

Additional documentation for medical justification includes photographs and videotapes (obtain patient consent), letters of support from related medical and educational institutions (e.g., teachers, occupational therapist, physical therapist, speech therapist, orthopedics), and information from the patient's medical chart. If a fire destroyed equipment, send documentation from the fire department. If a theft occurred, send documentation from the police department. Follow up with a second letter if additional information from the funding source is requested. Finally, if the request for funding is denied, and you still think the request is medically justifiable, have the patient request a fair hearing.

Please note that this sample letter is by no means the only correct way to construct a letter of medical justification. Its purpose is only to demonstrate the logical flow of information from patient evaluation to documentation in the form of a cogent letter for funding.

WHEELCHAIR FITTING

Once the wheelchair is ordered and delivered by the dealer, it should be properly fitted to the patient before it is dispensed. Note that several fittings may be required before the wheelchair is acceptable and ready for dispensing. Evaluate (1) the wheelchair, (2) the patient's positioning in the wheelchair, and (3) the caregiver's knowledge of the wheelchair.

1: Evaluate the Wheelchair

- *Is the order correct?*
- *Are all components in?* Go through the order with the dealer and check off each item ordered to determine if it was delivered.
- *Are postural supports installed securely?* Do not put the patient into the wheelchair unless you are sure it is properly secured.
- *Do all components operate* (e.g., removable parts, tilt mechanism)?
- *Do the wheel locks work?*

- *Does the wheelchair fold if it is supposed to?*
- *Is the frame stable* and are anti-tippers on the wheelchair, if ordered?
- *Are there any exposed sharp or hard edges* that can cause injuries?
- *Is the seat-to-back angle of the inserts acceptable* and set at the correct angle based on the patient's available hip flexion during the initial evaluation?

2: Evaluate Patient Positioning in the Wheelchair

First, properly place patient in wheelchair.
- *Are postural supports properly installed on the frame* based on the initial evaluation?
- *Is the seat depth acceptable?* There should be no more than 2 in. of space between the front of the seat and the back of the knees. No pressure should exist against the back of the knees.
- *Is the seat width acceptable?* Up to 1 in. of space on either side of the hips is acceptable.
- *Is the back height acceptable* based on patient activity level and sitting ability? The lower back (i.e., lumbar area) must be supported. If the patient self-propels, the backrest should not interfere with UE movements.
- *Is the foot plate height level acceptable?* The foot plate height should support the weight of the LE so that the thigh is approximately parallel with the seat cushion. If foot plates are adjusted too high, increased hip flexion

and excessive pressure under the ischia can develop. If foot plates are adjusted too low, excessive pressure under the distal posterior thigh can result.

- In the frontal plane, *is the pelvis (anterior superior iliac spines) level*, are the shoulders and eyes horizontal, and is the nose vertical? If the patient has a fixed scoliosis, are the head and shoulders balanced over the base of support?
- In the sagittal plane, *is the pelvis in a neutral tilt* with shoulder and head balanced over the pelvis?
- In the transverse plane, are the *pelvis, shoulders, and nose facing front* and not rotated left or right relative to the midline? If the patient has a fixed scoliosis, is the face facing front?
- *Are rear wheels ideally positioned* relative to the UEs? Determine if patient is most efficient in propelling when the wheel axes are aligned with or slightly in front of the patient's shoulder axes, and if the elbows are in a mild flexion (30 degrees) when the patient's hands reach to top of the rear wheels.
- Are *straps* and *seat belts* attached at the proper angles (typically 45 degrees for seat belts)?
- If a *chest harness* is used, is adequate clearance provided around the neck region?
- If a *pommel* is used, is it positioned distally, between the knees, and not proximally, into the groin?
- If *lateral trunk supports* are used, is there acceptable clearance of the axillary region with no pressure into the brachial plexus?

- If a *lap board* is used, is there sufficient space between the abdomen and the board for clothes and respiration?
- *Is the frame stable* when the patient is in the wheelchair?

3: Evaluate the Knowledge of Caregiver, Family, and Patients

Does the caregiver know how to do the following?
- Properly position the patient in the wheelchair
- Operate all the components (e.g., anti-tippers, wheel locks, armrests, front rigging)
- Fold the wheelchair
- Maintain the wheelchair
- Properly and safely position straps (harness) and supports
- Engage the wheel locks during transfers
- Negotiate curbs, ramps, and general maneuvering
- Follow up at the clinic if problems arise

SUMMARY OF EVALUATION QUESTIONS

The patient evaluation questions are summarized here for the clinician's convenience. The clinician can refer to detailed information concerning each question and its clinical importance in Chapters 2–4.

History

- Designate a spokesperson for the patient.
- What brought the patient to the clinic today?
- List problems with the existing wheelchair.

- Prioritize what is important to the patient.
- Discuss previous successes and failures.

Past Medical History

- Is there a diagnosis?
- What will the future bring?
- Are there plans for surgery?
- Is medication used that can impair judgment or level of consciousness or cause bleeding?
- Are there related medical problems?

Social History

- Where will the patient be living?
- Who will care for the patient?
- How does the patient spend the day?
- What does the patient want to do in life?

Indoors
- Door openings
- Clearance on turns
- Size of rooms
- Elevator or walk-up
- Storability

Outdoors
- Places, distances
- Terrain
- Transportation

Physical Examination

Passive Range of Motion

- Sufficient hip, knee, and ankle flexion to fit into a standard wheelchair?
- Neutral hip abduction, hip rotation, and subtalar positions possible?
- Spine straight and flexible?
- Sufficient UE range for propulsion?

Anthropometric Measurements

- For seat width, seat depth, back height, arm height, and knee-to-heel distances

Skin Integrity

- Existing or previous pressure sores

Sensation

- Does patient complain of pain when sitting?
- Does patient experience diminished position sense in the limbs?
- Does patient have impaired vision and hearing?

Postural Alignment

- Does patient sit symmetrically on request or with gentle force?
- Are fixed deformities present?

Active Movement

- Is any movement possible?
- Are movements rich and varied?
- Are movements functional?
- Can movements result in injury?
- Does the patient become stuck in one position?

Sitting Balance

- Can patient sit without external support?

Primitive Reflexes and Reactions[24]

- Asymmetric tonic neck reflex
- Symmetric tonic neck reflex
- Tonic labyrinth reflex
- Moro's reflex or startle reflex
- Positive and negative support reactions

Muscle Tone

- Is muscle tone extreme, persistent, high, low, or fluctuating?

Endurance and Speed

- Can functional distances be achieved by the patient?

Strength

- Is muscle strength adequate to perform wheelchair skills?

Motivation

- Is patient motivated to operate a wheelchair?

Judgment

- Does patient have sufficient judgment to use the wheelchair in a safe manner?

Memory

- Would the patient forget destinations or safe operation of equipment?

Vital Signs

- Does patient become dizzy when sitting upright or with changes in posture?

Body Shape

- Ectomorph, endomorph, mesomorph?

Patient Skills

Locomotion

- What can the patient do?
- Does the patient need a wheelchair?
- Can the patient propel a manual wheelchair?
- Is a motorized wheelchair a possibility?
- Is attendant assistance required to push a manual wheelchair?

Transfers

- What type of transfer will the patient be performing?

Sitting

- How much support is needed in sitting?
- What is the angle of comfortable gaze?

Upper Extremity Activities

- Does the patient have a functional reach?
- Can the patient self-propel using the upper limbs?
- Are the rear wheels ideally positioned?
- Does the patient self-feed?

EXERCISES

1. List and describe nine stages involved in wheelchair prescription.
2. What issue might you discuss with the caregiver or patient over the phone to prepare him or her for a wheelchair evaluation?
3. List at least 10 different types of wheelchair components that can be prescribed.
4. How might a clinician evaluate a patient for the following (e.g., focus of evaluation):
   a. mobility bases
   b. seat belts
   c. front rigging
   d. foot plates

    e. handrims

    f. rear wheels

    g. rear tires

    h. casters

    i. wheel locks

    j. armrests

    k. seat cushions

    l. seat inserts

  m. back inserts

    n. trunk supports

    o. head supports

5. List some features (options) for each of the following wheelchair components:

    a. mobility bases

    b. seat belts

    c. front rigging

    d. foot plates

    e. rear wheels

    f. rear tires

    g. casters

    h. handrims

    i. wheel locks

    j. armrests

    k. seat cushions

    l. seat inserts

  m. back inserts

    n. trunk supports

    o. head supports

6. Evaluation form
    a. How would you design your own wheelchair evaluation form to suit your needs in the clinic?
    b. What major headings would you include?
    c. Design an evaluation form and then compare yours to Form 1.1. (Did you leave anything out or would you include any additional information?)
7. Letter for medical justification
    a. What major headings would you include in a letter for medical justification?
    b. How could you further substantiate the medical necessity of a wheelchair for a client who was denied funding?
8. Describe an efficient sequence for conducting a wheelchair evaluation.

REFERENCES

1. Behrman AL. Clinical perspectives on wheelchair selection: factors in functional assessment. J Rehabil Res Dev 1990;2(suppl): 17–27.
2. Freney D. Pediatric seating. Home Health Care Dealer/Supplier 1995;Sept/Oct:103–105.
3. Taylor SJ. Evaluating the client with physical disabilities for wheelchair sitting. Am J Occup Ther 1987;41:711–716.
4. Wilson AB, McFarland SR. Types of wheelchairs. J Rehabil Res Dev 1990;2(suppl):104–116.
5. Redford JB. Seating and wheeled mobility in the disabled elderly population. Arch Phys Med Rehabil 1993;74:877–885.
6. Mattingly D. Wheelchair selection. Orthopaedic Nursing 1993;12: 11–17.
7. Eddy L. Physical Therapy Pharmacology. St. Louis: Mosby–Year Book, 1992;107–115.

8. American National Standard for Buildings and Facilities: Providing Accessibility and Usability for Physically Handicapped People. Accessible Elements and Spaces (A117.1). New York: American National Standard Institute, 1986;16–73.

9. Delisa JA, Greenberg S. Wheelchair prescription guidelines. Am Fam Physician 1982;24:145–150.

10. Grunewald J. Wheelchair selection from a nursing perspective. Rehabil Nurs 1986;11:31–32.

11. Rosenblith JF, Sims-Knight JE. In the Beginning: Development in the First Two Years. Newbury Park, CA: Sage, 1989;411–415.

12. Siev E, Freishtat B, Zoltan B. Perceptual and Cognitive Dysfunction in the Adult Stroke Patient: A Manual for Evaluation and Treatment (rev ed). Thorofare, NJ: Slack, 1986;53–87.

13. Kamenetz HL. The Wheelchair Book: Mobility for the Disabled. Springfield, IL: Thomas, 1969;132–134.

14. Ragnarsson KT. Clinical perspectives on wheelchair selection: prescription considerations and a comparison of conventional and light weight wheelchairs. J Rehabil Res Dev 1990;2(suppl): 8–16.

15. Miles-Tapping C, MacDonald LJ. Lifestyle implications of power mobility. Phys Occup Ther Geriatr 1994;12:31–49.

16. Harrymann SE, Warren LR. Positioning and Power Mobility. In G Church, S Glennen (eds), The Handbook of Assistive Technologies. San Diego: Singular, 1992;55–92.

17. Warren CG. Technical considerations: power mobility and its implications. J Rehabil Res Dev 1990;2(suppl):74–85.

18. Bergen AF, Presperin J, Tallman T. Positioning for Function: Wheelchairs and Other Assistive Technologies. Valhalla, NY: Valhalla Rehabilitation, 1990;13–62.

19. Kohlmeyer KM, Stevens S, Ueberfluss J. Wheelchairs. In GM Yarkony (ed), Spinal Cord Injury: Medical Management & Rehabilitation. Gaithersburg, MD: Aspen, 1994;169–172.

20. Currie DM, Hardwick K, Marburger RA, Britell CW. Wheelchair Prescription and Adaptive Seating. In JL Delisa, BM Gans (eds), Rehabilitation Medicine: Principles and Practice (2nd ed). Philadelphia: Lippincott, 1993;563–585.

21. Brant J. Wheelchair clinics work. Occup Ther Health Care 1988;5:67–70.

22. Garber SL. Classification of wheelchair cushions. Am J Occup Ther 1979;10:652–654.

23. Garber SL. Wheelchair cushions: a historical review. Am J Occup Ther 1985;39:453–459.

24. Fiorentino MR. Reflex Testing Method for Evaluating CNS Development. Springfield, IL: Thomas, 1981;14–21.

The Individual

Evaluate the patient first. Areas to address include patient history, physical impairments, patient skills, and body shape. These areas, which are reviewed in Chapters 2–4 and Appendixes 3 and 4, help determine the kind of wheelchair that can benefit the patient.

2

Patient History

What is the patient's story? Past and present problems provide information on what the patient may need in the future. Taking a history requires good listening skills.

SOURCE

Designate a Spokesperson for the Patient

Avoid a room full of people screaming to be heard. Instead, designate one spokesperson to provide relevant patient information. The spokesperson can be the patient, the legal guardian, or a family member. Other reliable persons can be interviewed later.

Who Should Be That Spokesperson?

The key is to talk to the person who spends the *most time* with the patient and therefore is familiar with the patient's lifestyle and behaviors. This can, of course, be the patient. If, however, the patient cannot communicate, the spokesperson can be a family member, long-time friend, home-health aide, or housekeeper.

- *Obtain the story from the right person.*

CHIEF COMPLAINT

What brought the patient to the clinic today? What is the chief problem? In other words, what motivated the patient or family to seek help? Write down this information. It will not only give the patient the feeling that someone is listening but will also help to focus on *problems important to the patient.*

PROBLEM LIST

List Problems with the Existing Wheelchair

Make a list of all patient and family concerns. Do not leave until all concerns are aired. Any injury-related concerns need to be addressed on the day of the clinic visit. Here are some of the more common wheelchair concerns:

- Patient is "uncomfortable" in wheelchair
- Patient slides out of wheelchair
- Head falls forward in the wheelchair
- Patient falls (listing) to the side
- Wheelchair tips over
- Patient "hooks" head around the headrest
- Patient injures self in the wheelchair
- Patient sits slumped in wheelchair
- Wheelchair is too small
- The wheel locks (brakes) are broken
- Wheelchair does not fold
- Wheelchair is difficult to push

Prioritize What Is Important to the Patient

Just because a clinician uncovered a problem, does not mean the patient's concerns were addressed in the clinic that day. Using a car repair analogy, you can bring your car to a mechanic with a noisy transmission problem, have a broken car door fixed, and leave with a noisy transmission. Make sure the patient's chief concern is addressed on the day of the clinic.

SUCCESSES AND FAILURES

What things have worked and failed in the past and present? Does the patient or family have any suggestions for successful future modifications?

There is no point in recommending something that has been previously tried and failed. If the patient has a new idea, hear him or her out. Patients and family members frequently have innovative and creative solutions to a problem. I once met a father who solved a front rigging problem on his daughter's wheelchair using plumbing pipe.

MEDICAL HISTORY

Next, obtain an idea of the patient's medical background, which is important when recommending a wheelchair.

Age

Anticipate growth in children when ordering a wheelchair. The average seating system sustains 2–3 years of child growth before a new seating system is needed.[1]

Gender

Men and women may differ in terms of their body fat distribution, limb length, and center of gravity. These factors, in turn, may affect their fit in a wheelchair (see Appendix 3).

Height

Tall patients may require a higher seat to facilitate transfers and clear feet from dragging on the floor.[2] Short-stature patients, on the other hand, may need a lower seat or a hemiplegic chair to facilitate transfers.[2,3]

Weight

Heavier patients (e.g., 250 lb) may exceed the weight limitation for which a standard wheelchair frame is guaranteed and may therefore require heavy-duty frame construction.

Diagnosis

Knowing the patient's diagnosis can help narrow your choice of wheelchairs. For example, a small premature infant who cannot self-propel a wheelchair may benefit from a stroller with adaptive inserts to provide postural support. A cardiac patient who sits well but has limited endurance may benefit from a motorized cart. A patient with hemiplegia, who is paralyzed on one side of his or her body, may benefit from a wheelchair with a seat that is low to the floor: The unaffected foot can then reach the floor to assist the patient in propelling the wheelchair. A nonambulatory patient with a severe scoliosis may need a seating system that is molded around the contours of the back deformity. Finally, a patient with a spinal cord injury who cannot use his or her arms or legs to self-propel can often benefit from a power wheelchair.

Wheelchair recommendations based on patient diagnosis are listed in the following sections. In practice, final recommendations *must* be based on a full evaluation of the patient by the team.

Obesity

The obese patient may require a wide, heavy-duty frame with shock absorption features to address body dimensions and weight limitations.

- Heavy-duty wheelchair (double cross-braced)
- Wide adult, oversized wheelchair (20 in. or wider)
- Extra long seat belt
- Full-length armrests to assist in transfers[2]
- Shock absorption features such as pneumatic (air) tires[4]

Undernutrition and Starvation

The thin, undernourished patient may need padding under straps, belts, and pressure reduction under ischia to address the potential for pressure sores.

- Padded straps and belts if used
- Pressure-reducing cushion

Arthrogryposis

The patient with arthrogryposis may need power mobility if upper extremity (UE) range of motion (ROM) restricts self-propulsion abilities. A molded back insert may be needed if significant spinal deformity is present.

- Power mobility if UE range is limited
- Custom-molded inserts for deformities

Head Injury (Severe)

Depending on the extent of involvement, the patient with a severe head injury may need postural support to maintain symmetric sitting, address the influence of abnormal tone or reflexes, and prevent contractures such as equinus deformities. The frame may need to be heavy duty if the patient is aggressive and applies excessive forces while in the wheelchair.

- Heavy-duty, strong frame
- Custom postural inserts
- Sufficient foot support to discourage risk of equinus deformity

Cerebrovascular Accident

The patient who had a stroke and has only one functional UE and lower extremity (LE) may need a hemiplegic or one-hand drive frame to self-propel. Brake extension on the involved side can facilitate reach to wheel locks. A lap board or support surface can help elevate an edematous hand, support a painful shoulder, or protect and enhance awareness of a neglected UE.

- Hemiplegia wheelchair
- One-hand drive mechanism frame
- Lap board
- Brake extension

Rheumatoid Arthritis

The patient with rheumatoid arthritis may benefit from a high seat to facilitate transfers, postural supports to rest involved body parts, large wheels to facilitate self-propulsion, and brake extensions to facilitate reach of wheel locks.[5]

- Higher seat
- Large rear wheels
- Elevating or removable leg rests if LE involvement
- Brake extensions
- Neck support piece if cervical involvement

Bilateral Lower Extremity Amputation

The patient with an amputation may need an amputee frame or amputee adapters to improve posterior stability and prevent backward tipping of the wheelchair, because these patients have a more posteriorly displaced center of gravity. The patient's residual limb lengths may be different and therefore require separate amounts of support on each side of the seat (i.e., split seat) for proper support.

- Amputee wheelchair

- Amputee adapter
- Split seat insert for below-knee amputee
- No front rigging for bilateral amputation[6] (unless prosthetics are used)

Quadriplegia

In general, patients with quadriplegia need a pressure-reducing cushion and a lightweight frame, if self-propulsion is possible, or a power wheelchair with power tilt and recline features and a back-up manual wheelchair, if mobility is limited.

C1–C4 Quadriplegia[7]

- Power wheelchair
- Pressure-reducing cushion
- Powered recline or tilt mechanism
- Back-up manual wheelchair[8]
- Life-support system (respirator) mounting[9] if needed

C5 Quadriplegia[7]

- Power wheelchair with hand controls
- Pressure-reducing cushion
- Back-up manual wheelchair[8] with oblique handrim projections[7]

C6 Quadriplegia

- Manual wheelchair, gloves, coated handrims, projections
- Power wheelchair for long distances and lifestyle needs

- Pressure-reducing cushion

C7–C8 Quadriplegia

- Manual wheelchair
- Pressure-reducing cushion

Paraplegia

The patient with paraplegia needs a pressure-reducing cushion and a lightweight or ultralight wheelchair to facilitate self-propulsion.

- Manual wheelchair (ultralight or lightweight)
- Pressure-reducing cushion
- Gloves to prevent friction burns from handrims

Triplegia

The patient with triplegia with only one functional UE may need a one-hand drive frame if hand function is adequate.[9] Postural alignment should be monitored, since there is a tendency for patients to lean to the side and out of midline to operate one-hand drive mechanisms.

- One-hand drive manual wheelchair

Myelomeningocele

The patient with myelomeningocele may need a molded back or pressure-relief area to accommodate spinal deformity. A pressure-reducing cushion can address a pressure sore risk due to lack of sensation, and an accommodating head-support shape may be needed for hydrocephalus if head control is poor.

- Manual wheelchair with growth capability
- Back insert with pressure relief for myelomeningocele
- Head support for hydrocephalus if needed
- Pressure-reducing cushion
- Seat covers for incontinence

Moderate-to-Severe Fixed Scoliosis

The nonambulatory patient with moderate-to-severe scoliosis may need a custom-molded back insert to accommodate spinal deformity.

- Custom-molded back insert

Hip Dislocation with Fixed Windswept Deformity

The patient with a hip dislocation and a fixed deformity may take up space in the wheelchair due to asymmetric sitting. The pelvis may be oblique, and LEs may both be deviated to the same side (i.e., windswept). A wider frame (to accommodate the windswept position) and a pressure-reducing cushion (to redistribute excessive weightbearing under the involved hip joint) may be required.

- Wider frame
- Pressure-reducing cushion

Cardiac Patient

Cardiac patients may need power mobility if there are exertion restrictions or endurance is severely compromised.

- Motorized cart (scooter)
- Power wheelchair

Self-Abusive Patient

The self-abusive patient may need a heavy-duty frame with padding on hard surfaces and nondetachable components to provide a safe environment.

- Nondetachable components (arms, front riggers, brake extensions)
- Heavy-duty frame if strong body activity
- Padding on hard surfaces at risk for injuring patient
- Anti-tippers if body rocking is evident

Seizure Disorder

Patients with a seizure disorder may require padding on hard surfaces, which may cause injury from impact during a seizure. Power mobility may be unsafe.

- Pad wheelchair components at risk for injuring patient

Total Hip Replacement

The patient with a total hip replacement may need a high seat level to discourage excessive hip flexion during transfer activities.[10] A pommel may help to prevent hip adduction while patient sits.

- Firm, thick cushion to transfer without leaning forward or increasing hip flexion
- Pommel

Geriatric Patient

A geriatric patient may need full-length adjustable armrests to facilitate transfers, a seat cushion to provide comfort or pressure reduction, and a curved back support to accommodate any fixed kyphotic spinal deformity.

- Adjustable height armrest to facilitate transfers
- Padded, wide, flat armrests[3]
- Curved back insert for fixed kyphosis
- Swing-away footrests for safe transfers
- Pressure-reducing seat cushion
- Seat covers for incontinence
- Consider restraint policies on positioning devices

Muscular Dystrophy

The patient with muscular dystrophy may need a lumbar pad and adjustable full-length armrests to support a lumbar lordosis if it exists.

- Lumbar support if excessive lordosis exists
- Full-length armrests for support of a lordosis[10]
- Growth capability in seat
- Adjustable height armrests for growth[6]

Cerebral Palsy

Depending of the degree of involvement, patients with cerebral palsy may need postural support to maintain symmetry, a tilt or reclined positioning for poor head control, a pressure-reducing cushion, and growth capability built into the wheelchair.

- Manual or power mobility
- Growth capability[1]: adjustable height armrests,[6] growth tail on seat insert
- Postural support: seat insert, back insert, lateral trunk supports
- Pressure-reducing cushion
- Seat covers if incontinent

Premature Infant with Neurologic Involvement (Cerebral Palsy)

The premature infant with neurologic insult may need postural inserts to prevent deformity and a stroller with growth capability for mobility.

- Stroller
- Postural inserts
- Growth capability[1]

Precautions

Determine if the patient is under any activity or positioning restrictions.[10] Two examples include restriction on self-propulsion for the severely compromised cardiac patient or avoidance of hip flexion for the patient with a recent total hip replacement. The former may need power mobility to minimize exertion, whereas the latter may need thick cushions to discourage excessive hip flexion.

Prognosis

Familiarize yourself with the progression of the disease.[10, 11] Will the patient make a quick, full recovery, require long-term care, or is he or she in the terminal stages of a disease? Renting a standard wheelchair may be sufficient for temporary use[10] if you anticipate the patient may not survive or alternatively will make a full recovery. For example, a patient with a fractured femur who needs a wheelchair to conserve energy or for safety during the healing process would rent. Such is also the case for a patient in the terminal stages of cancer.

On the other hand, purchasing a wheelchair can be appropriate if the patient's condition appears chronic. A child with cerebral palsy who does not walk will probably require long-term use of a wheelchair and may need custom-fitted postural seating inserts that can be adjusted for future body growth. Issues of durability and cosmesis become more important for long-term users of equipment.[10]

Finally, if the patient has a chronic, progressive, deteriorating disability, such as Huntington's disease or multiple sclerosis, purchasing a wheelchair that can be modified as the patient changes may be wise. Consider add-on components and the eventual possibility of power mobility.[10]

- Acute disability, short-term disability—rent
- End stages of terminal illness—rent
- Chronic disability—purchase

- Progressive deterioration—follow-up for needed modifications

Surgeries

Are there plans for surgery? Orthopedic surgery may alter the patient's anatomy. For example, surgical repair of a congenital hip dislocation can result in improved ROM or a change in leg length. It may be prudent to wait until after surgery to evaluate the patient for a wheelchair, because body shape and wheelchair needs may be different after the surgery.

- Surgery anticipated: consider postponing evaluation until after surgery
- No surgery anticipated: evaluate

Physical Rehabilitation

Is the patient making gains in therapy? If gains are being made in therapy, the patient may no longer need a special wheelchair feature or may not need a wheelchair at all in the near future. For example, if UE function for self-propulsion improves significantly, a manual wheelchair should be considered in lieu of a power wheelchair. Or, if sitting balance is improving from fair to good, lateral trunk supports may not be required in the near future. In each case, it may be sensible to wait until the patient's functional level plateaus before ordering the wheelchair.

Medications

Does the Patient Take Medication That Can Impair His or Her Judgment or Level of Consciousness?

Medication can affect patient performance in a wheelchair by altering level of consciousness, motor abilities, sensibilities, or endurance level. Patients who take medications that impair judgment should therefore be cautioned against operating a power wheelchair, just as individuals who take certain medications are cautioned against driving a car or operating machinery. Various drugs and their potential side effects are listed in the following sections.[12]

Antiepileptic Drugs

- *Phenobarbital*: sedation
- *Phenytoin* (Dilantin): visual, cerebellar-vestibular effects
- *Carbamazepine* (Tegretol): drowsiness, vertigo, ataxia, diplopia
- *Ethosuximide* (Zarontin): drowsiness, lethargy
- *Clonazepam* (Klonopin): drowsiness

Spasticity and Skeletal Muscle Relaxants

- *Baclofen*: drowsiness, muscle weakness
- *Chlorzoxazone*: sedation
- *Diazepam* (Valium): drowsiness

Antipsychotic Drug

- *Chlorpromazine* (Thorazine): extrapyramidal, muscle rigidity, tremors

Sedative-Hypnotics

- *Barbiturates*: drowsiness, central nervous system depression
- *Benzodiazepines*: drowsiness

In addition, the patient should be questioned regarding use of alcohol or nonprescription drugs that could impair judgment.

Medications That May Predispose Patient to Bleeding

- *Aspirin*
- *Heparin*
- *Warfarin sodium* (Coumadin)

Orthotics

Does the patient wear an orthosis? Orthotics, such as long leg braces and body jackets, take up space in a seating system and must be taken into account when measuring the patient for a wheelchair. Body jackets require additional seat depth. Long leg braces may require additional seat width.

- Measure the patient in the wheelchair with the orthosis.

SYSTEMS REVIEW

Are there related medical problems? Reviewing each organ system in the patient's body is a good way to cover "all the bases" and thereby reduce the chances of missing important information related to wheelchair needs. Thoroughness usually pays off in the end. To save time, this information can be found in the patient's medical chart. Alternatively, you can have the patient or family member fill out a form that includes the following information about related medical problems.

Congenital and Hereditary: Are There Skeletal Deformities?

The size of the patient's head may be hydrocephalic or microcephalic and require different size headrests. A child with spina bifida may have a congenital scoliosis that requires pressure relief around the back because of the associated back deformity. A child with a congenitally shortened leg length may require a seat cushion that is shorter on the involved side. A child with a congenital hip dislocation may need a seat cushion that provides sufficient pressure relief around the involved hip region.

- Hip dislocation: seat cushion for pressure relief around the head of the femur
- Scoliosis: custom-molded back insert to accommodate fixed deformity
- Leg length discrepancy: split-seat insert to accommodate a shorter thigh

Hematologic

Is There a Bleeding Disorder?

Bruising can occur when a patient's body part bumps into the metal component of the wheelchair. This is a particularly relevant issue in patients with low or inhibited platelet activity, such as occurs with hemophilia or thrombocytopenia.[12] Hard, exposed, wheelchair parts, such as front rigging, may require padding to minimize risk of future bruising.

Is There Anemia?

Patients with anemia can have limited endurance. Consider energy-conserving measures, such as use of lightweight frames or power mobility, to enhance independence if limitations are significant.

Cardiovascular

Is There Angina on Exertion or Shortness of Breath?

Self-propulsion may not be possible if UE activity precipitates symptoms such as angina. Consider energy-conserving measures such as power mobility.

Is There Lower-Limb Edema?

Edematous feet may take up space and may therefore require larger foot plates.

Pulmonary

Is Breathing Labored?

If manual propulsion is possible, consider energy-conserving measures such as a lightweight frame. Avoid excessive pressure from wheelchair components, such as chest harnesses or lateral trunk supports, which can interfere with rib and abdominal movements during breathing.

Is There a Tracheostomy Tube?

Keep the opening of the tracheostomy unobstructed. Wheelchair components, such as chest harnesses and straps, should be free from obstructing this opening. In addition, avoid positioning the patient's neck in excessive flexion, which can cause the chin to cover the tracheostomy opening.

Is Oxygen or a Ventilator in Use?

Consider attachment sites for this type of equipment on the wheelchair.[8]

Gastrointestinal

Is There Bowel Incontinence?

Consider fecal-resistant upholstery, such as vinyl, on the seat. Seat cushions that use open-cell foam allow penetration of liquids and should be covered with a protective, washable cover.

Is There Gastroesophageal Reflux?

If gastroesophageal reflux is present, a goal for the patient may be an upright seated position.[4]

Is There a Gastrostomy Tube?

Avoid pressure from seat belts and straps that may stretch or occlude the gastrostomy tube as it exits the patient's abdomen. Consider ordering and attaching a feeding pole to the wheelchair for patients who are continuously fed by a feeding tube.

Is There Weight Gain?

Patients may experience ascites, bloating, obesity, or organ enlargement. If the patient occupies a lot of space in a seat or is very heavy, consider width, depth, and strength requirements of the wheelchair. Make sure the manufacturer of the wheelchair frame guarantees the frame to withstand weight up to the client's body weight. Consider reclining the back a little to improve comfort and reduce pressure between the patient's thighs and abdomen if compression is present.

Is There Weight Loss?

Adipose tissue functions to pad bones. If the patient loses weight, adipose tissue is reduced and bony areas under pressure, such as the ischia, may be more susceptible to pressure sore development. Consider padding the metal portion of the seat belt buckle to avoid excessive pressure over bony pelvic areas such as the anterior superior iliac spine. Consider a pressure-reducing cushion for the ischia or greater trochanters.

Are There Weight Fluctuations Over Time?

If weight changes, be cautious about recommending custom-fitted components, such as molded-back inserts, which cannot be adjusted later. Custom-fitted components may fit well today but fit poorly next month after a weight change. In these cases, consider wheelchair components that are adjustable. For example, lateral trunk supports can be designed with knobs that can be adjusted in or out in width to accommodate changing trunk width.

Urologic

Is There Urinary Incontinence?

Consider urine-resistant upholstery, such as vinyl, over the seat cushion. Consider closed-cell foams that do not allow liquids (urine) to penetrate.

Is There Frequent Urination?

Consider wheelchair components, such as front rigging, armrests, and wheel locks, that are easy to manage for quick transfers to a toilet.

Are There External Urinary Bags, Tubes, or Catheters?

Avoid pressure from seat belts and straps at these sites, because pressure can occlude drainage from the tubing.

Gynecologic

If a patient is pregnant, consider accommodating short-term growth changes in the wheelchair. For example, consider extra-long seat belts as the pregnancy progresses. Order adjustable-height armrests to facilitate patient transfers in and out of the wheelchair.

Nutritional and Metabolic

If the patient has osteoporosis, avoid concentrated forces over bones that may lead to fractures. Ankle straps that secure a foot on a foot plate may result in excessive forces around the tibia if the patient pushes out against the strap. Consider padding a footbox to protect the feet from kicking activity, rather than using ankle straps if osteoporosis is present. Alternatively, distribute force over a larger surface area so that pressure is reduced in bony areas at risk of fracturing. During two-person maximal assisted transfers, consider having the patient wear a splint on body parts at risk of fracturing to reduce stress from the weight of the limb on the bones. These splints can be removed after the transfer.

Endocrine

Is There Diabetes?

Protect the patient from sustaining sores and cuts from wheelchair components, because wounds may heal poorly.[4]

Are There Associated Growth Disturbances?

Patients with short UEs may require a narrower frame, angling the wheels, rear wheels that are closer to the frame, or larger wheels to facilitate reach to the wheels for self-propulsion. On the other hand, patients with short LEs may require a frame that is low to the floor to facilitate transfers into the wheelchair.

Musculoskeletal and Connective Tissue

Are There Contractures?

Limited joint mobility in the hips and knees can prevent a patient from fitting in a standard wheelchair. If the patient has less than 90 degrees of hip flexion, the back of the frame may have to be reclined. If the patient has knee flexion contractures, the feet may need to be supported under the seat of the wheelchair. If the patient has an equinus deformity at the ankles, angle adjustable foot plates may be necessary to support the feet.

Is There Muscle, Joint, or Bone Pain?

If pain limits walking, a wheelchair may be needed for long-distance transportation.

Has the Patient Been Inactive or on Bed Rest?

Bed rest weakens most body systems, deconditions the cardiovascular system, and can lead to disuse atrophy in skeletal muscle. Muscle strength, endurance, and bone strength may be affected, resulting in deteriorated patient performance during transfers, walking, and wheelchair activities. If a new wheelchair is being considered, and you believe the patient's abilities will markedly improve, consider conducting the wheelchair evaluation after the patient is reconditioned and recovers from the effects of bed rest.

Neurologic

How Alert Is the Patient?

A diminished level of consciousness may not be compatible with safe, independent skills such as power mobility.

Are There Seizures?

If the patient has a seizure, he or she may lose control of motor abilities temporarily. Make sure the patient is adequately protected from injuries during uncontrolled movements of body parts while in the wheelchair. Power mobility may not be a safe option in wheelchair mobility in patients who have seizures (e.g., petit mal, grand mal).

Is There Sensory Loss?

Consider using materials, such as foams and gels, that help distribute pressure in areas that are insensate and therefore have the potential for skin breakdown.

Is There Uncontrolled Movement?

Try to anticipate sites of potential injuries as a result of uncontrolled head, trunk, upper limb, or lower limb movements. Uncontrolled movements that lead to asymmetric postures need to be corrected with postural support.

Is There the Potential for Nonverbal Communication?

Consider consulting with a communication specialist (e.g., occupational therapist or speech therapist) for appropriate technology that can be used while the patient is in the wheelchair.[13]

Does Patient Have Problems with Drooling?

Consider easy-to-clean fabrics for upholstery, straps, and chest harness materials. Consider consulting with a speech therapist to improve patient's ability to swallow saliva.

Is There a Temperature Regulation Problem?

If the patient experiences fluctuations in body temperature, make sure there is sufficient space in the wheelchair for periodic use or removal of additional clothing, blankets, or thermal equipment. Note that custom-molded seating systems closely fit around the patient and may not offer sufficient space for additional clothing.

Psychiatric and Psychological

Is the Patient a Danger to Him- or Herself or Others?

Consider nonremovable armrests, brake extensions, and front rigging, so these wheelchair components cannot be used as weapons.

Is There Self-Abuse?

Protect the patient from harm by padding or removing hard or sharp components. For example, if the patient bangs his or her head into the lap tray, the tray should either be padded or discontinued.

Are There Other Behavioral Problems?

If the patient can walk but refuses, a wheelchair may be necessary for transportation to clinics and school. Parents, for example, may complain of how their child will sit or fall to the ground and refuse to walk any further. On further examination, callused or bruised knees may be noted as a result of repeated falls to the ground.

Are There Specific Restraint Policies Where the Patient Resides?

In nursing homes, equipment such as seat belts and lap trays may not be permitted on a patient's wheelchair if the equipment prevents the patient from getting out of the wheelchair independently. Check with the residence if restraint policies prohibit the use of positioning equipment.

Dermatologic

Is there contact dermatitis? Certain materials, such as industrial chemicals and metals, can cause a skin reaction or rash in the patient when they contact the skin. Commonly affected skin areas include the face, neck, hands, legs, and feet. Avoid materials (i.e., metals, fabrics) that the patient is hypersensitive to, or cover these parts during wheelchair construction.[14]

SOCIAL HISTORY

Lifestyle

Where Will the Patient Live?

The patient's residence must be wheelchair accessible. A patient who lives in a house or apartment may need ramps, a wider door, and other modifications to access the home. A patient who lives in a facility may already have full access to all areas in the building. Hallways need to be wide enough to allow the wheelchair to turn around a corner. Bathroom doorways need to be wide enough to access a rolling commode chair. Tables need to be high enough to allow the patient's knees to fit under the table.

- Facilities may be wheelchair accessible.
- Private houses and apartments may have architectural barriers and require planning for narrow, light, or folding type wheelchairs.

Who Will Care for the Patient?

As a general rule, the more people involved in the patient's care, the more difficult it is to take care of a patient's property, such as a wheelchair. If many people take care of the patient (e.g., three nursing shifts, school, bus driver), there is a good chance wheelchair components will become lost. Consider placing the patient's name on all removable parts. Try to minimize the number of components that can be removed from the wheelchair to minimize loss. Teach all persons involved in the patient's care how to use the wheelchair properly. If the patient lives alone, consider equipment that does not require a high level of maintenance.

- *Patient lives alone*: Order low-maintenance equipment.[11]
- *Many people involved in care*: Train all caregivers in care of equipment. Place name labels on equipment.

Next, try to gain a sense of who the patient is (as a person!) and what he or she has been doing in life up to the time of the clinic visit.

How Many Hours Does the Patient Spend in a Wheelchair?

Break down the patient's day into thirds and determine how the patient's morning, afternoon, and evening are spent. How many rest periods does the patient need out of the wheelchair? Does the patient stay in bed most of the time or stay in the wheelchair all day long? If the patient spends a minimal amount of time in a wheelchair, customized postural supports may not be crucial. On the other hand, if the patient spends many hours in a wheelchair, a pressure-reducing cushion and postural supports become increasingly important to prevent deformity and pressure sores.

- *Minimal time in wheelchair*: Custom postural support may not be critical.
- *Many hours in wheelchair*: Pressure-reducing cushion and postural support become increasingly important.

What Limitations Does the Patient Experience in the Present Wheelchair?

This question immediately places the patient's problems into a meaningful or functional context. For example, does the patient need a standing frame to perform duties at work, a power wheelchair to travel very long distances, or a power tilt-in-space mechanism to provide rest periods so that long hours at a job can be tolerated?

Indoor and Outdoor Environments

Will the Patient Spend Most of the Time Indoors or Outdoors?

A patient who mostly remains indoors will deal with a less physically and perceptually demanding environment. On the other hand, the patient who ventures outdoors must deal with a more challenging and less predictable environment, such as oncoming cars, uneven terrain, and changing weather conditions.[15]

Indoors

Patients *may not* require a heavy-duty wheelchair if it will only be used indoors and the patient is not rough on the frame. Determine if the patient's home is wheelchair accessible (Figure 2.1). Have the patient or family draw a layout of the home if important room, corridor, or furniture dimensions are not clear.

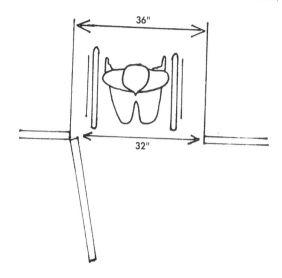

Fig. 2.1 Wheelchair accessibility. A 32-in. doorway and 36-in. corridor clearance is sufficient for most wheelchairs. Determine maximal doorway clearance with the door opened by measuring from the door jamb on one side (vertical side frame of the door) to the inside corner of the door.

Door Openings

Measure the maximum width of door openings to ensure that the wheelchair and lap board, if used, can fit through doorways. The recommended doorway clearance needed for a standard wheelchair is 32 in.[16] This amount of clearance should be sufficient for a 26-in.–wide standard adult wheelchair. Bathroom doorways are typically too narrow for a wheelchair.

- Recommended door opening clearance: 32 in.[16, 17]
- Standard wheelchair width: 26 in.[16]

Corridors

Measure corridor width to determine if a wheelchair has sufficient width for passage.

- Minimal passage width for one wheelchair: 36 in. (32 in. to pass a short distance)[16]
- Minimal passage width for two wheelchairs: 60 in.[16]
- Minimal width for one ambulatory individual to pass one wheelchair: 48 in.[16]

Clearance on Turns

Make sure that the wheelchair has enough room to make a turn (180-degree angle) in a narrow hallway. Turning requires an area with a 60-in. diameter.[16] The longer a wheelchair frame, the more difficult it is to negotiate turns in a narrow hallway. Turns are more difficult if elevated legrests are used, since they make the wheelchair longer.

- Turning space required for a standard wheelchair: 60-in. diameter[16]

Work Surfaces

Measure work-surface height for clearance of knees under the work surface. Work surfaces need to be at least 27 in. from the floor to clear the knee of an individual in a standard adult wheelchair. More knee clearance may be needed if thicker seat cushions are used or the seat level is raised.

- Height of tables: range from 28 in. to 34 in. from floor[16] (for standard wheelchair)
- Knee clearance: at least 27 in. (height) × 30 in. (width) × 19 in. (depth)[16]

Bed Height
Determine the difference between wheelchair seat height and bed height.[10] The seat level on a standard adult wheelchair is 19 in.[16] A seat cushion, however, can raise the seat height. A hospital bed with adjustable height features may be able to level the bed mattress to the same height of the seat cushion to facilitate sliding board transfers.

Floor Surface
If floors are carpeted, consider pneumatic tires and casters to reduce rolling resistance of the wheelchair.[11] For hard surfaces, solid tires are adequate.

Size of Rooms
Bedrooms should have adequate space to maneuver a wheelchair around in preparation for transfers. The minimal space required for one stationary wheelchair and user is 30 in. × 48 in.,[16] but additional space will be required to maneuver.

Elevator or Stairs

If the elevator is frequently out of order and the family lives on a high floor, the family may need to carry the wheelchair up several flights of stairs. Consider a lighter weight wheelchair or a stroller for these patients. Minimal elevator dimensions to fit a standard wheelchair are 51 in. × 36 in.[16]

Small Living Spaces

If there is limited space in the home, order a wheelchair that folds to take up less space. The width of a folded standard adult wheelchair is 11 in.[17] Consider ordering an indoor wheelchair with large wheels in the front for better maneuverability in small living spaces.

Architectural Barriers in the Home

Consider the following options if a wheelchair is required but the home is not accessible:

- Order the narrowest frame width acceptable for a particular patient to clear doorway openings.
- Order a lightweight frame (or appropriate size stroller with postural inserts if patient does not self-propel) to carry on stairs.
- Order detachable components to make wheelchair lighter while carrying on stairs.
- If patient does not self-propel, remove handrims to clear doorway openings.
- Order wrap-around or fixed (nonremovable) armrests to minimize width.

- Do not angle the rear wheels, to minimize width.
- Order a narrowing device to temporarily narrow frame width to clear doorways.
- Order a folding frame to clear doorway openings with patient out of wheelchair.
- Adapt the home or find accessible housing.
- Refer to social worker for housing assistance.

Outdoors

Stronger wheelchair construction is generally recommended for rugged outdoor use. Consider having the patient or family draw a map of the neighborhood, including important places and distances (city blocks). The following areas may be included.

- *Destinations*: What are important destinations for the patient (e.g., bus stop, work, bank, grocery store, restaurants, clinic, school, park)?
- *Distances*: How far must the patient travel to important destinations?
- *Time*: How much time does it take to reach a destination?
- *Type of terrain*: The type of wheelchair construction (i.e., standard, lightweight, heavy duty) and tires are determined in part by where the wheelchair will be used.
  Bumpy terrain[11] (e.g., grass, gravel): Consider pneumatic or wide tires for greater shock absorption; heavy-duty, strong frame construction; and large casters to negotiate over cracks.

Broken glass: Consider airless tires for maintenance-free care.

Hilly terrain: Consider a lightweight manual frame; make sure power wheelchairs can negotiate steep hills. Grade-aid wheel locks may help patients negotiate up hills in a manual wheelchair.

Inclines: To prevent backward tipping while propping up on inclines, consider anti-tippers, a long anterior-posterior frame base of support, an amputee frame, or a posterior rear wheel axial position.[11]

Ramps: Minimal width for standard wheelchair clearance on ramps is 36 in.[16] Please note that ramps on vans may be only 31 in. wide or less. (I have received plenty of complaints when patients who were fitted in wide wheelchairs could not fit on the van ramps.)

How Will the Patient Be Transported?

If the patient uses the bus, make sure the wheelchair is narrow enough to access the ramp and low enough for the patient and wheelchair to clear the top of the bus door. Also make sure the wheelchair is capable of being secured (tied down) to the floor of the bus properly for safety. Consider the use of a headrest (removable) to reduce risk of whiplash in a wheelchair during bus travel.

If the patient travels by car or taxi, make sure the wheelchair folds easily and consider removable rear wheels (quick-release wheels) to make the wheelchair smaller for storage during transportation.

Funding Source

Explore all potential funding sources with a social worker, because wheelchair recommendations may ultimately be limited by available funds.[10]

EXERCISES

1. Discuss prescription considerations based on patient age, gender, body weight, and height.
2. What kind of wheelchair prescription might a clinician first consider for the following diagnoses?
   a. C5 quadriplegia
   b. cerebrovascular accident
   c. amputation
   d. paraplegia
   e. self-abusive patient
3. What medications might interfere with a patient's safe operation of power mobility?
4. Conduct a systems review and consider how each system can impact your decision to prescribe a wheelchair.
5. How would a patient with an acute, chronic, or progressive condition affect your decision to prescribe a wheelchair?

REFERENCES

1. Freney D. Pediatric seating. Home Health Care Dealer/Supplier 1995;Sept/Oct:103–105.
2. Wilson AB, McFarland SR. Types of wheelchairs. J Rehabil Res Dev 1990;2(suppl):104–116.

3. Redford JB. Seating and wheeled mobility in the disabled elderly population. Arch Phys Med Rehabil 1993;74:877–885.

4. Currie DM, Hardwick K, Marburger RA, Britell CW. Wheelchair Prescription and Adaptive Seating. In JL Delisa, BM Gans (eds), Rehabilitation Medicine: Principles and Practice (2nd ed). Philadelphia: Lippincott, 1993;563–585.

5. Brattström M, Brattström H, Eklöf M, Fredström J. The rheumatoid patient in need of a wheelchair. Scand J Rehabil Med 1981;13:39–43.

6. Bergen AF, Presperin J, Tallman T. Positioning for Function: Wheelchairs and Other Assistive Technologies. Valhalla, NY: Valhalla Rehabilitation, 1990;13–82.

7. Kohlmeyer KM, Yarkony GM. Functional Outcomes After Spinal Cord Injury Rehabilitation. In GM Yarkony (ed), Spinal Cord Injury: Medical Management and Rehabilitation. Gaithersburg, MD: Aspen, 1994;9–14.

8. Warren CG. Technical considerations: power mobility and its implications. J Rehabil Res Dev 1990;2(suppl):74–85.

9. Ragnarsson KT. Clinical perspectives on wheelchair selection: prescription considerations and a comparison of conventional and light weight wheelchairs. J Rehabil Res Dev 1990;2(suppl):8–16.

10. Mattingly D. Wheelchair selection. Orthopaedic Nursing 1993;12:11–17.

11. Behrman AL. Clinical perspectives on wheelchair selection: factors in functional assessment. J Rehabil Res Dev 1990;2(suppl):17–27.

12. Eddy L. Physical Therapy Pharmacology. St. Louis: Mosby–Year Book, 1992;73–79, 107–125.

13. Taylor SJ. Evaluating the client with physical disabilities for wheelchair sitting. Am J Occup Ther 1987;41:711–716.

14. Marino MA, Vivio SDR. Care of Children with Physical and Emotional Problems. In B Christensen, E Kockrow (eds), Foundations of Nursing. St. Louis: Mosby, 1995;1369–1446.

15. Poulton EC. On prediction in skilled movements. Psychol Bull 1957;54:467–478.

16. American National Standard for Buildings and Facilities: Providing Accessibility and Usability for Physically Handicapped People. Accessible Elements and Spaces (A117.1). New York: American National Standard Institute, 1986;16–73.

17. Olson SC, Meredith DK. Wheelchair Interiors. Chicago: National Easter Seal Society for Crippled Children and Adults, 1973;3–16.

3

Physical Examination

Physical impairments resulting from disease can affect how the patient functions in a wheelchair. For example, limited hip joint extension is an impairment that affects a patient's ability to sit. Upper extremity (UE) muscle weakness is an impairment that can affect the patient's ability to propel a wheelchair.

The physical examination focuses on physical impairments related to the patient's ability to function from a sitting position. The first part of the examination can be performed while the patient is safely positioned in sitting. Postural alignment, active movements, sitting balance, muscle tone, endurance, speed, strength, perception, and cognitive status can be assessed. The second part of the examination can then be performed on the mat, so that passive range of motion (PROM), anthropometric measurements, skin status, and sensation can be recorded.

POSTURAL ALIGNMENT

Good posture can be viewed as the position of maximal function. From an evolutionary perspective, good posture may be the position from which the individual can respond equally well from all directions and with the least amount of energy.[1] For example, consider sitting in a chair with the intention of standing up to avoid danger. You will be in a better sitting posture to quickly stand and move in any direction and with less preparation if your feet are first both planted on the floor instead of resting under the chair.

Most of us function best when we are symmetric. When symmetry is possible, our joints are not in extreme positions, our muscles are not working excessively to keep us upright, and we can perform movements to a similar extent on either side of the body. When symmetry is not possible due to deformity, try to support the patient so that his or her head balances in midline over his or her pelvis.

Step 1: Does the Patient Sit Symmetrically?

Observe how the patient typically sits. Check if the patient can maintain a balanced or symmetric sitting posture with eyes horizontal, nose vertical, shoulders level, and pelvis level. (Physical therapists are really into being symmetric. I know one therapist who desires to be buried symmetrically.)

Step 2: Is the Patient Positioned to the Rear of the Seat?

Ask the patient or assist the patient to sit toward the rear of the seat so that his or her posterior pelvic area is contacting the back of the wheelchair. You can visually confirm that the patient's posterior pelvic area is touching the back of the wheelchair by having the patient lean his or her trunk forward so that the position of his or her posterior pelvis can be inspected.

Step 3: Ask the Patient to Assume a Symmetric Sitting Posture

Once the patient's pelvis is to the rear of the seat, determine if the patient can voluntarily sit symmetrically without support.

Step 4: Can Correction Be Attained with Gentle Force Using External Supports?

If the patient cannot sit voluntarily without support, but is flexible (i.e., easily bends without discomfort) in the neck, trunk, and pelvis, then symmetric sitting may be possible using postural supports. Equipment, however, should be used judiciously, because some patients may hang over postural supports rather than rely on themselves to balance and sit straight.

Step 5: If Fixed Deformities are Present, Decide on the Optimal Position for Patient Function and Accommodate Support Around this Fixed Position

If fixed deformities and asymmetries are present, such as scoliosis or dislocated hips, determine which body part should be oriented toward the patient's environment. Should the patient's head, shoulders, pelvis, knees, or feet face front? If fixed rotational deformities are present, it is not possible to have all body parts face front.

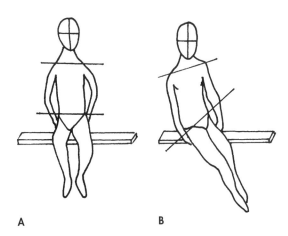

A   **B**

Fig. 3.1 A. Symmetric sitting with nose vertical, eyes horizontal, and shoulders and iliac crests level. B. In patients with fixed asymmetric deformity, the head is balanced over the support base with eyes horizontal and nose vertical.

One approach is to balance the head and trunk over the pelvis. Head and shoulders should be level and facing front if possible so that the eyes are horizontal and the nose is vertical (Figure 3.1).[2,3] The sense organs for vision, hearing, taste, smell, and touch are located in the head and should be oriented toward the patient's environment (facing front). Remaining body parts, such as the pelvis, hips, knees, and feet, should then be supported in whatever posture they are fixed. *Avoid excessive weightbearing over one ischium or greater trochanter* when attempting to bal-

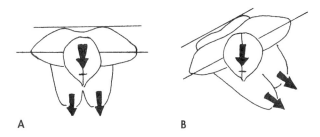

Fig. 3.2 A. Patient is symmetric with head, shoulders, and hips facing front. B. Patient exhibits a fixed windswept deformity and must have hips positioned out of midline so that the head can remain facing front.

ance the patient's head and shoulders over an inflexible pelvis, because it may lead to a pressure sore.

Patients with scoliosis may have to position their lower limbs in a windswept position (both knees deviated off to the same side) so that their head and eyes can face front (Figure 3.2). *It is important* that the patient and family are prepared for this approach, because existing deformities may become more apparent.

ACTIVE MOVEMENT

Is Any Movement Possible?

If the patient does not move at all, there is a great risk for skin breakdown because weight shifting, which relieves pressure, is not possible. Teach weight-shifting activities to patients who can move, or have the patient's position changed periodically by the caregivers if the patient cannot move. Consider a pressure-reducing seat cushion for patients who cannot move. Reclining and tilt-in-space wheelchair frames can also help to shift the patient's weightbearing area in the seat.[4]

If Movement Is Not Possible

- Attendant-assisted pressure relief every hour for 30 seconds[5]
- Independent weight shifts using a power tilt or recline on frame[6]

If Movement Is Possible

- Teach independent pressure relief every 15[7] to 30 minutes[5] for 15 seconds.

If the Patient Is Active, Are Movements Rich and Varied?

One of the hallmarks of physical disability, especially with brain damage, is a reduction in the richness or variety of voluntary movements, which able-bodied individuals normally possess. The repeated uncontrolled hip adduction in cerebral palsy or the persistently flexed posture of the patient with Parkinson's disease are common examples of the poverty of movement in patients with central nervous system involvement. Although movement variety may be small, some voluntary movements can be put to good use. Determine what movements are possible for the patient and then attempt to assist the patient in using these movements to function independently.

Are Functional and Reliable Movements Possible?

Determine what useful movements are consistently within the patient's repertoire. For example, could the patient's hands or feet be used to propel the wheelchair if the wheel was closer to the hand or the seat lower to the floor? Could the patient open and fasten the seat belt if an airplane-type belt was provided? Could a patient with only head movement adopt a more independent lifestyle if a switch was strategically placed on a headrest to permit power wheelchair operation? Note that patients with only $\frac{3}{16}$ of an inch of available movement can be able to operate a switch on a power wheelchair.[6]

Maximize the Function Potential of Reliable Movements

Maximize the function potential of reliable movements using assistive technologies and switches.[6] Consult with an occupational therapist and assistive technology expert.

Are One to Two Body Movements Possible for Operating Switches for a Power Wheelchair?[6]

- Lip control
- Tongue control
- Puff or sip control
- Chin control

- Headrest control
- Joy stick
- Arm or elbow control
- Shoulder position
- Knee control
- Foot control

Can Patient Movements Result in Injury?

Not all movements are functional. The problem is when the patient experiences movement-related injuries while in a wheelchair. Injuries, for example, are prevalent in patients with Huntington's disease because of their involuntary movements.

Before dispensing the wheelchair, determine if any body segment is at risk for injury. *Methodically* review the patient's head, neck, trunk, and upper and lower limb movement patterns to determine if any of these moving body segments can potentially result in wheelchair-related injuries or fatalities. Pad components, block movement that can result in injury, and inspect the patient's environment for hazardous conditions (e.g., stairs).

Observe Body Areas at Risk of Injury

Observe body areas at risk of injury from head to toe.

- The *head* can become caught around a headrest if the patient tends to list his or her trunk to the side of the headrest.

- The *neck* can become hung up in the chest harness if the patient has poor sitting balance and slides forward in the wheelchair.
- *Fingers* can become caught in the wheelchair spokes.
- The *trunk* can become bruised from leaning over the armrest in a patient with poor sitting balance.
- The *feet* can fall off the foot plate and drag the ground.
- The wheelchair may tip backwards or sideways.
- Inspect the environment for high-risk areas.

Environmental Factors Related to Wheelchair-Related Fatalities[8]

- Stairs (most common)
- Bathroom
- Ramps
- Water-related
- Automobile
- Curb
- Elevator, train tracks, garage door

Injuries Associated with Wheelchair-Related Fatalities[8]

- Skeletal (most common), especially femoral fractures
- Respiratory
- Central nervous system
- Cardiovascular
- Integumentary, gastrointestinal, genitourinary

Does Patient Become Stuck in One Position?

Can the patient safely move into and out of a position without help? It may be acceptable for a patient to hook his or her head around the side of the headrest and then return to the original position but not acceptable if he or she is stuck in that position for an hour. At issue is whether the patient lacks a choice in movements and subsequently becomes stuck in a dangerous position. If the patient cannot reverse the direction of a movement, then consider blocking (stopping) that movement with adaptive equipment, such as lateral trunk supports, until the patient can achieve better control.

Are There Upper Extremity Degenerative Changes?

Long-term use of a wheelchair can lead to wear-and-tear (repetitive) UE injuries such as osteoarthritis, rotator cuff injuries, bursitis, and tenosynovitis.[9]

SITTING BALANCE

Can the Patient Sit Without External Support?

Determine if the patient sits safely under static and dynamic conditions, because both may be encountered during a patient's day. Can the patient respond quickly to a perturbation or is the response too slow or delayed to be of safe functional value. If responses to static or dynamic perturbations are inadequate, postural supports, such as a chest harness or lateral trunk supports, may be necessary for safety.

Static Sitting Balance

Static sitting balance is determined by having the patient short sit with feet supported on the floor while the patient is adequately guarded by someone. Explain the procedure to the patient and then gently push the patient in anterior, posterior, and lateral directions while observing how the patient recovers from the perturbation. Can the patient maintain his or her eyes and shoulders horizontal during the perturbation, or do the patient's head and trunk list uncontrollably to the side? Can the patient recover from the perturbation without assistance from the clinician?

Alternatively, have the patient sit on a base that tilts and perturb the base of support to observe how the patient recovers when suddenly moved (i.e., this test may simulate balance demands in a moving vehicle such as a bus).

Dynamic Sitting Balance

Dynamic sitting balance is determined by having the patient short sit as above and actively reach for objects in different directions, such as toward the floor, the sides, and to the rear. Can the patient propel a wheelchair while maintaining trunk balance? The clinician observes if the patient can shift weight to reach for the object and then recover to a midline position without loss of balance.

Protective Extension Reactions

Does the patient exhibit protective extension reactions by reaching out to the support surface with the arms to break a fall or protect the head?

PRIMITIVE REFLEXES AND REACTIONS

Does Sensory Stimulation Result in Stereotypic Motor Responses?

The patient's positioning in the wheelchair can be negatively affected by primitive reflex activity (Figures 3.3 and 3.4).[10] Try to identify the stimulus that triggers an undesirable response and control the response using adaptive equipment if possible. For example, if an asymmetric tonic neck reflex (ATNR) causes the patient to assume an asymmetrical "fencing" posture every time the head rotates out of midline, consider a headrest with a side panel to block and discourage head rotation to that side (if tolerated) while in the wheelchair. Note that primitive reflexes can indirectly affect pelvic position, resulting in forward sliding activity.

Asymmetric Tonic Neck Reflex[10]

Head rotation can result in the following (see Figure 3.3):

- Limb extension and trunk convexity on the side of head rotation
- Asymmetric sitting, which promotes a scoliotic posture

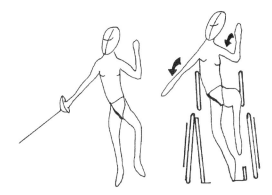

Fig. 3.3   Patients who exhibit an asymmetric tonic neck reflex assume a "fencing" posture and tend to place excessive pressure under one buttock in a wheelchair.

- Excessive asymmetric weightbearing with risk of pressure sore over one ischium or hip

Symmetric Tonic Neck Reflex[10]

Head flexion or extension can result in the following:

- Lower extremity (LE) extension with UE flexion when head flexes (Figure 3.4A)
- LE flexion with UE extension when head extends (Figure 3.4B)
- Forward sliding in wheelchair
- Sacral sitting with risk of sacral or coccyx pressure sore

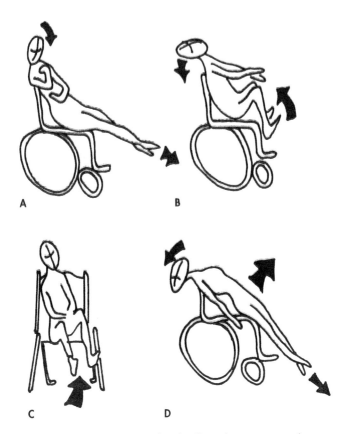

Fig. 3.4 Primitive reflexes can indirectly affect pelvic position, resulting in forward sliding activity. A. Symmetric tonic neck reflex (with cervical flexion). B. Symmetric tonic neck reflex (with cervical extension). C. Negative support reaction. D. Tonic labyrinth reflex.

Tonic Labyrinth Reflex[10]

Reclining the backrest may result in the following (see Figure 3.4D):

- Extension of trunk and extremities
- Forward sliding in wheelchair
- Sacral sitting with risk of sacral or coccyx pressure sore

Patients who exhibit a tonic labyrinth reflex when reclined in a wheelchair may assume a strong extensor pattern in the trunk and extremities. Patients may tend to "pop out" of the wheelchair and demonstrate forward sliding behavior.

Moro's Reflex and Startle Reflex[10]

Sudden head extension or loud noise can result in the following:

- Alternating extension-flexion extremity movements
- Forward sliding in wheelchair

Positive Support Reaction[10]

Foot stimulation can result in the following:

- Strong extension of LEs
- Standing on, and possibly bending, front rigging

Negative Support Reaction[10]

Patients who exhibit a negative support reaction may tend to withdraw their LEs into flexion when their feet contact the front rigging. These patients may have difficulty resting their feet on the foot plates. In addition, hyperflexion at the hips may pull on the hamstrings and result in posterior tilting of the pelvis with sacral sitting.

Foot stimulation may result in the following (see Figure 3.4C):

- Strong flexion of LEs
- Posterior pelvic tilt
- Sliding, sacral sitting with risk of sacral or coccyx pressure sore
- Feet may not remain on foot plates

MUSCLE TONE

Normally, muscle tone, the readiness of muscle to move, changes according to the demands of a task. Clinicians should start to be concerned when muscle tone becomes inappropriately high, low, persistent, or fluctuating to the point that it interferes with the patient's ability to function. Evaluate the patient under different gravitational conditions, such as upright sitting, supine, reclined sitting, and backward-tilted sitting, to determine the effect of tone on patient alignment and ability to function. Note that a patient may exhibit high tone in some body parts (e.g., limbs) and low tone in other areas (e.g., trunk).

If Muscle Tone Is Excessively High

The patient may have difficulty relaxing into the seat of the wheelchair if muscle tone is excessively high. These patients tend to be rough on wheelchairs and tend to wear, bend, or break wheelchair components. Consider reinforcing wheelchair components that have been previously broken due to patient force. (I have seen several patients with severe extensor tone at the neck break headrests repeatedly.) Try to position patients so that excessive tone is reduced. For example, excessive LE extensor tone may be reduced in some patients if the hips are placed in flexion and abduction while sitting. A wide pommel placed between the knees can help maintain this tone-reducing position.

If Muscle Tone Is Excessively Low

Patients with low tone may collapse their trunk into gravity while sitting upright and may have the feel of a rag doll when passively moved. These patients are very difficult to support in an upright position and may require gravity-assisted sitting using a tilt or a reclined wheelchair frame.

If Muscle Tone Fluctuates

If muscle tone fluctuates (i.e., tone changes from high to low), the constant movements associated with the tone changes can result in pelvic movements and eventual sliding problems for the patient. Try to adequately stabilize the patient's pelvis with a seat belt secured across the hips to control patient sliding.

Muscle Tone Summary

- *High flexor tone*: Trunk may pitch forward, or knees may raise up toward the chest while in wheelchair.
- *High extensor tone*: Pelvis may thrust forward, and patient may tend to stand up from wheelchair; frame may break or bend.
- *Low tone*: Trunk may collapse into flexion.
- *Fluctuating tone*: Patient may tend to slide forward in wheelchair.
- *High tone secondary to spasticity*: Bumpy terrain may "set off" involuntary movement, altering position in wheelchair, and making operation of a power wheelchair difficult.[11]

PASSIVE RANGE OF MOTION

Wheelchairs are generally designed for people who do not have difficulty bending the hips, knees, and ankle joints. In other words, to fit in a standard wheelchair, the patient must be able to bend his or her body into the shape of a chair.

Is Flexibility Sufficient to Fit in Wheelchair?

Standard wheelchairs require that patients have at least 90 degrees of hip flexion, a 70-degree popliteal angle at the knee (i.e., –70 degrees from full knee extension with hips in 90 degrees of flexion), and a neutral ankle position.[2] If the patient lacks this joint flexibility, then poor sitting alignment, poor sitting tolerance, sliding problems, and pressure sores could result if the patient is placed in a standard frame.

Check for flexibility:

- 90 degrees of hip flexion
- 70-degree popliteal angles
- Neutral ankle dorsiflexion

To determine if the patient has sufficient range of motion (ROM) to sit upright in a standard wheelchair, do the following three steps.

Step 1

First, place the patient in supine and gently flex both hips in the direction of the chest with the knees flexed so that the hamstring muscles are placed on slack.[12] Carefully watch when the coccyx lifts off the mat. If both hips can flex to a 90-degree angle so that the thighs point toward the ceiling while the coccyx remains on the mat, then the patient can probably fit in a standard wheelchair.

If, however, the patient's coccyx lifts off the mat *before* the hips reach 90 degrees (while the knees are flexed), then hip flexibility is probably inadequate for a standard wheelchair (Figure 3.5). A reclining wheelchair or a wheelchair with a seat-to-back angle adjusted to an angle greater than 90 degrees may be necessary. Placing a patient who exhibits hip flexion restrictions into a standard wheelchair causes the patient to sacral sit and slide forward in the wheelchair.

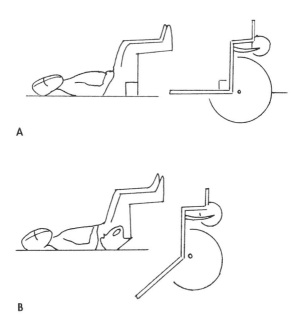

Fig. 3.5 A. Patients need 90 degrees of hip flexion to fit into a standard wheelchair. B. A patient who exhibits only 60 degrees of hip flexion does not have sufficient flexibility to sit upright in a standard frame and needs either a reclining frame or an open seat-to-back wheelchair angle (i.e., greater than 90 degrees).

Step 2

Next, determine if the patient has sufficient hamstring length to use standard 70-degree front rigging. In supine, maintain the patient's hips in 90 degrees if available and then slowly extend both knees so that the legs make a 70-degree angle with the vertical (i.e., 70-degree popliteal angles) (Figure 3.6B).

If knee flexion contractures or hamstring tightness is present and the knees cannot be extended with the hips flexed, then the feet may need to be positioned with 90-degree front rigging (Figure 3.6A) or underneath the wheelchair to accommodate the knee flexion contracture (Figure 3.6C). On the other hand, if knee extension contractures are present and the knees cannot flex, then an elevating legrest may be needed to support the legs.

Step 3

Finally, check if the ankles can be dorsiflexed to a right angle when the knees are flexed. If the ankles are able to bend so that the foot can rest flat on a surface, then a standard set of foot plates may be adequate (Figure 3.7A). If, however, an equinus deformity is present, then special foot plates with angle-adjustable capability may be needed (Figure 3.7B).

Remaining Lower Extremity Range of Motion

Are hip abduction, neutral hip rotation, and neutral subtalar positions possible in sitting? Correct to neutral if flexible. Otherwise, accommodate fixed deformities.

- *Hip adduction contractures* narrow the patient's sitting base and increase instability.

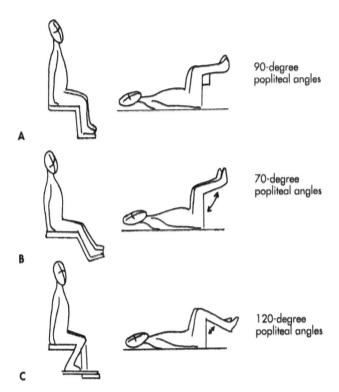

90-degree
popliteal angles

A

70-degree
popliteal angles

B

120-degree
popliteal angles

C

Fig. 3.6 A. Patients with tight hamstrings, exhibiting only 90-degree popliteal angles, may need to have their knees positioned with 90-degree front rigging. B. Patients who have adequate hamstring length, exhibiting 70-degree popliteal angles, may be able to use standard front rigging in a wheelchair. C. Patients who exhibit severe knee flexion contractures (e.g., 120-degree popliteal angles) may need their knees positioned in flexion with their feet supported underneath the wheelchair.

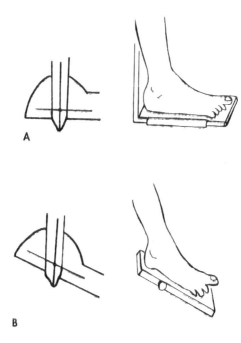

Fig. 3.7 A. Patients with neutral ankle range of motion can be supported by standard foot plates. B. Patients with a fixed equinus deformity may need adjustable foot plates to accommodate the ankle joint restriction.

- *Windswept hip position* may require a wider frame because widest seat-width measurements are now recorded from one hip to the contralateral knee (Figure 3.8).

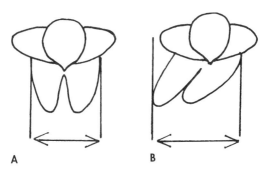

Fig. 3.8   A. Patient is symmetric and seat width is based on distance from hip to hip. B. Patients with a fixed windswept deformity sit with one hip adducted and the other hip abducted and may need a wider seat.

- *Inverted and everted foot positions* can cause excessive pressure over the lateral or medial border of the foot, respectively.

Upper Extremity Range of Motion

Is UE ROM sufficient to self-propel a wheelchair?

- *Wrist flexion contractures* limit grasp ability of hand-rims.
- *Elbow flexion contractures*[13] restrict reach of rear wheels and forward wheelchair propulsion.
- *Frozen shoulders* can interfere with UE flexion or extension phases of wheelchair propulsion.

The Spine

Is the spine straight and flexible? When we were young, grown-ups told us to sit up straight. This, however, is only possible if our spine is flexible enough. Determine if the patient's trunk is flexible or fixed by visually inspecting alignment or applying gentle tension to the spine.

First Approach: Visually Inspect Trunk Alignment

Step 1
First, level the pelvis so that both anterior superior iliac spine landmarks are on the horizontal plane.

Step 2
Then, with the pelvis maintained in this level position, try to gently level the shoulders so that both acromial processes are also on a horizontal plane. If a level shoulder position cannot be attained, then the spine may not be flexible enough to permit symmetric sitting. If an optimal symmetric posture cannot be attained, try to at least balance the patient's head in midline over the patient's support base (the pelvis). A molded back insert can accommodate a fixed spinal deformity in a wheelchair.

Second Approach: Apply Tension to Spine

You may also assess spinal flexibility by applying *gentle tension* to the spine while the patient is sitting by gently leaning the patient forward in sitting. Check if the patient's back looks symmetric or if there is a rib hump or hollow area on either side.

If the spine is not straight or if the back does not appear symmetric, refer the patient for medical evaluation to rule out scoliosis. An orthopedic referral is particularly important if the patient is still young and growing, because the risk of curve progression is greater in this population.

ANTHROPOMETRIC MEASUREMENTS

Measure the patient's body dimensions in supine and sitting to determine the proper wheelchair size (Figure 3.9).

Position the patient in supine with the hips and knees in 90 degrees of flexion[12] or in sitting on a firm surface with feet support on a flat surface (e.g., floor). Note that measurements may be different in sitting and supine because of the gravitational effects on the trunk.

Measure the patient more than once to ensure reliable records. Also, measure the patient wearing all orthotics and prosthetics if in use. Account for seat cushion height (i.e., usually 2 in.) and any postural support pieces, such as hip guides and lateral trunk supports, that can add width to the client in the wheelchair (i.e., usually 1 in. per side).[14,15]

Seat Height

Seat height is the measurement from floor to seat (i.e., from bottom of the heel to the posterior thigh)[15] plus an additional 2 in. to account for foot plate height from the floor.

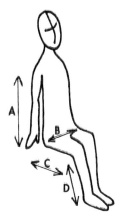

Fig. 3.9 To determine wheelchair size, measure (A) back height, (B) seat width, (C) seat depth, and (D) leg length from knee to heel on the patient.

Seat Width

Seat width is the measurement from hip to hip plus an additional 2 in. If the patient does not require postural supports to address deformity[16] and a close fit is desired,[12] seat width measurement may be the distance between the patient's greater trochanters (i.e., distance between seat rail). Orthotics, hip guides, thicker winter clothing, and anticipated weight gains, however, may require the additional seat width.[12] A patient who is windswept at the hips may also require additional seat width. Regardless of the patient's situation, hips should not be laterally compressed by the sides of the wheelchair (see Figure3.9B).[16]

Seat Depth

Seat depth is the measurement from front of the seat (back of knee) to the back of the pelvis (with the pelvis touching the back of the chair). Subtract up to 2 in. from the measurement to provide clearance between the front of the seat and the back of the knee. Measure each leg individually if a femoral leg length discrepancy exists. The front edge of the seat should be *no more than 2 in.* from the popliteal crease after the patient is properly positioned (see Figure 3.9C).[16]

Back Height

Back height is the measurement from the seat to that level on the patient's back that offers sufficient back support (i.e., typically to the inferior angle of scapula, lower if trunk control is good and higher if additional spinal support is required) (see Figure 3.9A).[16]

Leg Length

Leg length is the measurement from the seat (cushion) to the foot plate. If a leg length discrepancy exists between tibias, measure each leg individually so that each foot can be supported at different levels (see Figure 3.9D).

Arm Height

Arm height, which determines armrest height, is measured from the seat to the elbow (with the scapula relaxed, arm vertical, forearm flexed to 90 degrees, and forearm pronated). Then add an additional 1 in. to the measurement, so that the upper limb is adequately supported. Excessive armrest height, however, can result in scapula elevation, which should be avoided because it can affect UE function and posture. Account for seat cushion thickness when measuring armrest height because it adds height to the seat.[15]

Additional Measurements

Additional measurements can be useful if you are measuring for other components such as placement of lateral trunk supports (chest width), harness size (i.e., trunk width and length), head supports (i.e., head width and length), or foot plate size (i.e., foot length).

SKIN

Is Skin Intact?

Skin is our body's first line of defense against infection. With the patient's permission, inspect all bony areas of the body that are at risk of pressure sore development from prolonged or excessive weightbearing while sitting. Red areas that remain visible for more than 30 minutes are at risk for skin breakdown and should be relieved from pressure until normal skin color returns.[5]

- *Compromised areas* are red areas remaining visible for more than 30 minutes.[5]

Inspect for:

- Red coloration
- Bruises
- Breaks in skin
- Old, healed, pressure sore areas
- Graft sites[13]

Risk Factors for Pressure Sores[17]

- Diagnosis (e.g., spinal cord injury)
- Limited UE function
- Postural deformity
- Number of hours in wheelchair
- Types of activities
- Terrain
- Climate (temperature, humidity)
- Level of independence or inactivity
- History of tissue compromises
- Incontinence
- Sitting pressures and distribution
- Body build (i.e., thin patients)[18]

- Poor nutrition
- Excessive perspiration

Risk Areas

The following *bony* weightbearing areas are risk areas for pressure sores:

- Ischia
- Coccyx
- Greater trochanters
- Spinous processes
- Scapula
- Ears
- Back of head
- Elbows
- Knees
- Ankles and heels

Reducing Pressure

Areas at risk should be provided with pressure reduction by removing the local pressure source or distributing the pressure over a greater surface area in the following ways:

- Shaping the support surface
- Using pressure-reducing seat cushion materials (e.g., foams, air, gel)
- Using dynamic seating (power operated)

- Altering weightbearing areas within the frame by using a recline or tilt-in-space frame
- Teaching active weight shifting to the patient
- Instructing the caregiver to periodically lift the patient from the seat surface to temporarily relieve the continuous source of pressure
- Altering risk factors (e.g., terrain, nutrition, climate, hours sitting, activity level)

Are There Lumps, Bumps, or Bruises?

Skin markings can suggest rubbing or a repeatedly injured body part. Lumps can suggest inflammation, cysts, or tumors. Check for calluses on the knees or elbows for indications of excessive weightbearing in these areas. Check for bruising on the upper or lower limbs resulting from banging into metal or hard wheelchair components. Check for masses (cysts) on or below the skin that may require pressure relief in the seating system. Refer questionable surface injuries and masses for medical evaluation. Report suspected signs of child abuse to the appropriate agency. Inspect for the following:

- *Callused areas*: Provide pressure relief.
- *Bruised areas*: Provide padding.
- *Prominent bony areas*: Cut out a pressure-relief area.
- *Masses*: Refer for medical evaluation.
- *Suspicious signs of child abuse*: Report to the appropriate state agency.

SENSATION

Does the Patient Cry or Complain of Discomfort When Sitting?

If yes, the good news is that the patient may be sensate and capable of feeling pain. Pain is an important warning signal that tissue damage may be occurring. The ability to adjust position due to discomfort is dependent on intact sensation.[13]

Pain sensation can be tested using a sterile disposable safety pin and asking the patient to report sharp and dull.[19] Please note that the patient may still retain light-touch sensation as assessed with cotton and yet be anesthetic to pain because different neurotracts mediate pain and light touch. Examine anesthetic areas on the patient that contact the backrest, seat, and footrest for signs of impending pressure sores.

Is Position Sense Diminished in the Limbs?

Position sense (i.e., the ability to know the location of a limb in space without vision), is important for motor control.[20] Position sense can be tested by having the patient attempt to reproduce a passively displaced limb position without the aid of vision. If the patient lacks position sense of a limb, he or she may need to rely on vision to perform motor tasks such as propelling the wheels, operating the wheel locks, or adjusting the footrest. If vision is necessary to compensate for diminished position sense, make sure the patient's vision is not obstructed by equipment.

Is Vision or Hearing Impaired?

Visual problems significantly limit independent self-mobility, because the patient is not able to see where he or she is going. Consider referral for an eye evaluation and possible eyeglasses to improve vision. If the patient has diminished hearing, warning sounds, such as sirens, conversation, and instructional efforts, may not be appreciated, and the patient may feel isolated. Consider a referral for an auditory evaluation and possible hearing aids. Note any visual or hearing deficits, such as the following:

- Blindness
- Peripheral vision deficits
- Hemianopsia (field cuts)
- Hearing impairment

ENDURANCE AND SPEED: FUNCTIONAL DISTANCE

Functional distance is a relative measure and depends on where the patient needs to go and when he or she wants to get there. How far can the patient propel a wheelchair? Is this a meaningful distance for the patient in his or her particular neighborhood (i.e., going to work, to the bus, to the store, into an elevator, crossing a street)? Reporting that the patient can propel 150 feet is not as meaningful as stating that the patient can propel 150 feet to the corner drugstore and back within 15 minutes without assistance. Measure how many feet the client can self-propel to a destination and how many minutes it takes to reach the destination. If endurance is very limited or the patient is a marginal wheelchair user, consider a lighter weight manual frame or power mobility.

STRENGTH

Many wheelchair skills require applying forces against gravity, such as lifting wheelchair components having mass (e.g., front rigging), or propelling wheels that offer resistance to rolling. Most skills performed under gravity require muscle grades to be *greater than fair*. Note that spasticity, although not a measure of muscle strength, is sometimes used by patients to perform skills such as adjusting sitting posture or transferring out of a wheelchair.

Is adequate strength available in the upper limbs

- To shift body weight sideways to perform a pressure-relieving push up?
- To propel the wheels?
- To stop the wheelchair?
- To engage the wheel locks?
- To lift a front rigging or armrest?

Is strength adequate in the lower limbs

- To propel the wheelchair with the feet?
- To lift the foot onto the foot plate?
- To assist in transfers out of the wheelchair?

COGNITION: INTENTIONAL BEHAVIOR

Does the patient exhibit intentional behavior? Normally, means-end behavior, or the ability to use a means to achieve an end, is attained within the first 2 years of development[21] (Piaget's sensorimotor period). An example of this behavior is pulling on a string to acquire a toy. Acquisition of this behavior is required to problem solve and intentionally act on the environment and is therefore required to operate power mobility or even a manual wheelchair.

PERCEPTION[22]

Do perceptual deficits affect wheelchair mobility or safety? Note if the patient has figure ground, unilateral neglect, or depth perception deficits.

- *Figure ground*: Can foreground (people) be distinguished from background?
- *Unilateral neglect*: Does the patient bump into objects and people on one side of the environment or consistently turn the wheelchair in one direction only?
- *Depth perception*: Is depth misjudged (e.g., on stairs, curbs, and architectural barriers)?

MOTIVATION

Is the patient motivated to operate a wheelchair? To do anything voluntarily, there must be adequate emotional drive from the limbic system of the brain. If the patient has no desire to move, there will be no movement. A patient's power wheelchair may end up in a closet, never to be used, if the patient is not motivated to use it in the first place. Try to provide a sufficient trial period to determine if equipment will be used by the patient.

- *Motivated*: Encourage independence.
- *Unmotivated*: Allow a sufficient trial period; re-evaluate goals; refer to psychologist if patient appears depressed.

JUDGMENT

Is judgment adequate for independent wheelchair use? A safety issue can arise if the patient is motivated but lacks judgment. A wheelchair provides mobility, which can bring the patient close to a danger, such as thermal sources in a kitchen, stairwells in a building, or traffic at an intersection. Judgment needs to be assessed in the real-life context in which the wheelchair is used.

- *Good judgment*: Encourage independent mobility.
- *Poor judgment*: Encourage limited independence[23] and safe, supervised, or limited mobility. Keep away from stairways.

MEMORY

Patients with impaired memory may not remember how to return to their room from the physical therapy or occupational department. The patient with a memory deficit may not therefore be a candidate for unsupervised manual or power mobility.

For patients with poor memory:

- Encourage supervised mobility.[23]
- Provide identification for patient and wheelchair.

VITAL FUNCTIONS

Is orthostatic hypotension present? A patient may not be able to tolerate upright sitting or transfer to a wheelchair safely if bouts of dizziness occur as a result of a drop in blood pressure. Measure blood pressure changes from lying to sitting. If a drop in systolic blood pressure greater than 20 mm Hg occurs on sitting up, consider the following strategies:

- Gradual change in position
- Reclining backrest or backwards tilting frame to enable the head of the patient to be lowered to improve sitting tolerance
- Using elevating legrests to reduce pooling of fluid
- Referring for medical evaluation

GENERAL AND LOCAL BODY SHAPE

(See Appendixes 3 and 4.) Consider body shape issues that can impact wheelchair selection.[24, 25]

EXERCISES

1. Try to view a friend's body segment three dimensionally while he or she sits. For example, for the shoulder,

determine if the shoulders are level or if one side is higher or lower when *viewed from the front*. Next, determine if the shoulders both face front or if one is rotated more forward or backwards when *viewed from above (aerial view)*. Finally, determine if the shoulders are aligned directly over the hips or if they are too far forward or backward when *viewed from the side*.

Repeat this exercise with the pelvis. These exercises can be done with most body parts to determine how symmetric and balanced the segment is in space.

2. What are the critical ROM measurements at the hip, knee, and ankle to fit into a standard wheelchair?
3. Name at least five risk factors for developing a pressure sore.
4. How would you define "good posture"?
5. Is it more important to have a large amount or a reliable amount of movement to operate the controls of a power wheelchair?
6. What anthropometric measurements are needed to prescribe a frame size?
7. Practice taking anthropometric measurements on a friend in both the sitting and supine position. How do measurements of back height and seat width taken in the two positions compare?
8. How would patients with either high or low muscle tone influence your decision to order a wheelchair?
9. Would a custom-molded back insert be appropriate for a patient who has a functional scoliosis that is flexible and correctable to neutral?

10. What is the most hazardous environmental factor related to wheelchair fatalities?
11. Your patient assumes a persistent fencing posture while sitting in a wheelchair. What pathologic reflex causes this posturing and what problems is it associated with?

REFERENCES

1. Feldenkrais M. Body and Mature Behavior: A Study of Anxiety, Sex, Gravitation, and Learning. New York: International University Press, 1949;66–78.
2. Taylor SJ. Evaluating the client with physical disabilities for wheelchair sitting. Am J Occup Ther 1987;41:711–716.
3. Grunewald J. Wheelchair selection from a nursing perspective. Rehabil Nurs 1986;11:31–32.
4. Currie DM, Hardwick K, Marburger RA, Britell CW. Wheelchair Prescription and Adaptive Seating. In JL Delisa, BM Gans (eds), Rehabilitation Medicine: Principles and Practice (2nd ed). Philadelphia: Lippincott, 1993;563–585.
5. Donovan WH, Dinh TA, Garber SL, et al. Pressure Ulcers. In JL Delisa, BM Gans (eds), Rehabilitation Medicine: Principles and Practice (2nd ed). Philadelphia: Lippincott, 1993;716–732.
6. Warren CG. Technical Considerations: Power Mobility and Its Implications. J Rehabil Res Dev 1990;2(suppl):74–85.
7. Panel for the Prediction and Prevention of Pressure Ulcers in Adults. Pressure Ulcers in Adults: Prediction and Prevention. Clinical Practice Guideline, no. 3. AHCPR pub no. 92-0047. Rockville, MD: Agency for Health Care Policy and Research, Public Health Service, U.S. Department of Health and Human Services, 1992;5.
8. Calder CJ, Kirby RL. Fatal wheelchair-related accidents in the United States. Am J Phys Med Rehabil 1990;69:184–190.
9. Ragnarsson KT. Clinical perspectives on wheelchair selection: prescription considerations and a comparison of conventional and light weight wheelchairs. J Rehabil Res Dev 1990;2(suppl):8–16.
10. Fiorentino MR. Reflex Testing Methods For Evaluating CNS Development (2nd ed). Springfield, IL: Thomas, 1981;14–21.

11. Ozer MN. Clinical perspectives on wheelchair selection: a participatory planning process for wheelchair selection. J Rehabil Res Dev 1990;2(suppl):31–36.

12. Bergen AF, Presperin J, Tallman T. Positioning for Function: Wheelchairs and Other Assistive Technologies. Valhalla, NY: Valhalla Rehabilitation Publications, 1990;13–82.

13. Behrman AL. Clinical perspectives on wheelchair selection: factors in functional assessment. J Rehabil Res Dev 1990;2(suppl):17–27.

14. Kamenetz HL. The Wheelchair Book: Mobility for the Disabled. Springfield, IL: Thomas, 1969;128–134.

15. Delisa JA, Greenberg S. Wheelchair prescription guidelines. Am Fam Physician 1982;24:145–150.

16. Brubaker C. Ergonometric considerations. J Rehabil Res Dev 1990;2(suppl):37–48.

17. Garber SL. Wheelchair cushions: a historical review. Am J Occup Ther 1985;39:453–459.

18. Garber SL, Krouskop TA. Body build and its relationship to pressure distribution in the seated wheelchair patient. Arch Phys Med Rehabil 1982;63:17–20.

19. Swartz MH. Textbook of Physical Diagnosis: History and Examination. Philadelphia: Saunders, 1989;457–520.

20. Magill RA. Motor Learning: Concepts and Applications (4th ed). Madison, WI: WCB Brown and Benchmark, 1993;96.

21. Rosenblith JF, Sims-Knight JE. In the Beginning: Development in the First Two Years. Newbury Park, CA: Sage, 1989;411–415.

22. Siev E, Freishtat B, Zoltan B. Perceptual and Cognitive Dysfunction in the Adult Stroke Patient: A Manual for Evaluation and Treatment (rev ed). Thorofare, NJ: Slack, 1986;53–87.

23. Mattingly D. Wheelchair selection. Orthop Nursing 1993;12:11–17.

24. Sheldon WH. The Varieties of Human Physique: An Introduction to Constitution Psychology. New York: Harper, 1940;1–9.

25. Tortora PG, Eubank K. Survey of Historic Costume: A History of Western Dress (2nd ed). New York: Fairchild Publications, 1994;304–305.

4

Patient Skills

Patient skills are another area to consider when determining wheelchair needs. These skills include locomotion, transfers, sitting, and upper limb abilities.

- *The key question to ask: What can the patient do?*

LOCOMOTION

Does the Patient Need a Wheelchair?

If the patient is a functional ambulator, safely ambulates to required destinations without help (i.e., with or without assistive device and bracing), and can keep up with his or her peers, then a wheelchair is not needed. Consider a wheelchair if the patient cannot safely ambulate or if ambulation is limited to short distances.

If a Wheelchair Is Needed ...

Can the Patient Self-Propel a Manual Wheelchair?

If the patient cannot functionally walk, determine if self-propelling a manual wheelchair is possible using the upper or lower extremities.[1]

If the patient uses his or her upper extremities to self-propel, consider a back insert that permits trunk extension mobility during self-propulsion. If the patient uses his or her legs to self-propel, consider a low seat with the front of the seat beveled (undercut) so that the backs of the patient's knees do not hit the front edge of the seat as the feet pull under the wheelchair. Also remember that some patients may be more functional by propelling the wheelchair backward using their feet.

Is Use of a Power Wheelchair Possible?

If the patient cannot functionally walk or self-propel a manual wheelchair but can be safe and independent using a power wheelchair, consider an evaluation and trial for power mobility. Much thought must go into a power wheelchair recommendation, because the patient's community (e.g., home, streets, school, bus, stores) must be accessible, and the power wheelchair must be maintained.

Curiously, little has been published concerning guidelines for prescribing power wheelchairs.[2] Patients should be evaluated for (1) a postural support system, (2) type of mobility base, and (3) type of controls. The patient should be evaluated *in* a power wheelchair to determine functional ability, placement of controls, and safety under similar home environment conditions. Judgment, perception, means-ends behavior, and some reliable movement to operate the controls are required. The patient needs to stop when intended, slow down near doors, and look left and right to avoid hazards.[2] Determine if the patient can safely negotiate straight paths, turns, elevators, ramps, door openings, crowds, and outdoor terrain.

If Attendant Assistance Is Needed

If the patient cannot walk, self-propel a manual wheelchair, or safely operate a power wheelchair, consider attendant assistance to push a manual wheelchair. Consider the attendant's (pusher's) needs when recommending a manual wheelchair (i.e., wheelchair weight, push handle height).

TRANSFERS

Determine what type of transfers the patient will be performing, so that appropriate wheelchair features can be recommended to aid the patient in transferring. Remember, wheel locks must be engaged for safety regardless of the type of transfer.

If the patient can transfer independently, the patient should be able to manage all wheelchair parts. Make sure wheelchair components, such as seat belts, armrests, wheel locks, and front rigging, can be independently removed and reattached.

Stand-Pivot Transfers

If the patient can stand up and pivot during transfers, make sure armrests are of adequate height and length to assist in standing, wheel locks on both sides of the wheelchair can be reached, and front rigging can swing away (i.e., swing-away footrests) so that the patient or assistant does not trip over the foot plates during the transfer.

Equipment Considerations

- Height-adjustable, full-length armrests
- Swing-away front rigging
- Accessible wheel-lock location

Sliding Board Transfers

If the patient can use a sliding board (i.e., is able to slide sideways from a wheelchair to a bed using a shellacked wood board), make sure armrests are removable so that the sliding board can be properly placed under the patient's buttocks. The seat surface should also be stable enough during the transfer. Seat cushion material made with foam may be stable, whereas air-bladder cushions may be less stable.

Equipment Considerations

- Removable armrests
- Stable seat insert surface

Forward Transfers

Forward transfers, which are commonly performed by patients with bilateral lower limb amputations, enable the patient to transfer out of the wheelchair by positioning the front of the seat flush with the bed and scooting forward. If the patient has front rigging, make sure he or she can swing it completely away from the front of the wheel-chair so that the seat can be positioned flush with and per-pendicular to the bed.

Equipment Considerations

- Swing-away or detachable front rigging

Two-Person Transfers

If the patient depends totally on others to be lifted, make sure armrests are removable so that caregivers do not have to lift the patient any higher than necessary over obstacles (i.e., the armrests) during the transfer. Removable headrests and swing-away front rigging enable caregivers to exercise better body mechanics by standing closer to patient (i.e., the load).

Equipment Considerations

- Removable armrests
- Swing-away front rigging
- Removable headrests

Mechanical Lift Transfers

If the patient is too difficult or too heavy to transfer safely with manual help, consider a mechanical lift. Check that the patient's weight is within the lift's weight limit. Confirm that the patient has sufficient space at home to store the lift. Make sure the base of the lift can fit around the wheelchair so that the patient can be moved directly over the seat and then properly lowered into the wheelchair. Also make sure everyone is trained to use the lift, since tipping and injuries can occur if the lift is not properly used or the patient is not properly positioned in the lift's sling.

Equipment Considerations

- Lift guaranteed to support patient's weight
- Proper training of caregiver
- Sufficient room in the home for the lift

Car Transfers

If patient lifts his or her wheelchair into a car, consider the following features to make the lift more manageable.

Equipment Considerations

- Folding frame
- Lightweight frame
- Handle on wheelchair to pull and lift wheelchair into car[1]
- Removable armrests
- Swing-away front rigging
- Removable postural inserts

SITTING

How Much Back Support Is Needed?

Determine how much support the patient requires in sitting. Activity level and sitting balance determine how much back support is needed (Figure 4.1).

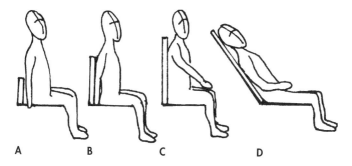

Fig. 4.1 Back support height is determined by the amount of trunk control and activity level. A. Low back support provides minimal support for very active patients with good trunk control. B. Middle back support provides postural support for the trunk while still allowing unrestricted use of upper extremities during self-propulsion. C. High back support provides maximal postural support for the trunk but can interfere with upper extremity self-propulsion. D. Patients using reclining or tilt wheelchairs need full head and trunk support.

Low Back Support

If the patient is very active (in sports) and needs minimal support to sit, a *low back height* is least restrictive and permits trunk bending, extension, and turning. Note that back support that is too low can result in back pain (Figure 4.1A).

Middle Back Support

If the patient self-propels but needs additional trunk support (usually the case), consider a *middle back height* (just below the scapula) so that arm, scapula, and upper trunk movements are unrestricted during wheelchair propulsion (Figure 4.1B).

High Back Support

If the patient has poor trunk control and does not self-propel, consider a *higher back height* (to acromial level) (Figure 4.1C).

Higher Back Support and Head Support

Finally, if the patient has poor head control, a *higher back and a headrest* may be necessary (Figure 4.1D).

Back Height Needs[3]

- *Good trunk control*: to inferior angle of scapula
- *Fair trunk control*: to shoulder height
- *Poor trunk and head control*: total back and headrest support

Determine Head Position for a Comfortable Eye Gaze

Normally, with the head vertical, the eyes can gaze comfortably down at objects up to 30 degrees below the horizon.[4]

UPPER LIMB FUNCTION

Functional Reach

Does the patient have a functional reach? Limited functional reach (e.g., how far patients can reach to greet people, open doors, push elevator buttons, or retrieve objects from the floor) is an important problem for wheelchair-dependent patients.[5, 6] Evaluate forward and sideways reach abilities of the patient while in the wheelchair. Make sure the wheelchair is stable both forward and sideways in patients who reach during activities of daily living or sports. Note that wheelchair components, such as lap boards, chest harnesses, and seat belts, can restrict the patient's reach ability.

Reaching Distances

- *High forward reach*: 48 in. from floor (required to reach elevator buttons[6])
- *High side reach*: up to 54 in. above floor[6]
- *Low forward reach*: no less than 15 in. above floor recommended[6]
- *Low side reach*: no less than 9 in. above floor recommended[6]
- *Backward reach*: toward utility bag hanging from the back of the wheelchair

Self-Propelling Using the Upper Limbs

Can the patient self-propel using his or her upper limbs? If the patient self-propels, determine if the patient can reach toward rear wheels; grasp the handrims; and start, stop, and maneuver the wheelchair forward, backward, on turns, through doorways, on ramps, on elevators, and outdoors. Popping wheelies (i.e., balancing the wheelchair on the rear wheels only) is a more advanced wheelchair skill used for quick turning and independent curb negotiation.

Wheel Position

Are rear wheels ideally positioned? If the patient can self-propel, make sure the rear wheel axles are ideally positioned relative to the patient's shoulder joint so that the patient can reach the top of the handrim at the beginning of the push. If the rear wheels are not positioned optimally relative to the patient, wheelchair propulsion efficiency can suffer. The patient has a biomechanical advantage if his or her muscles are at resting lengths.[7] However, the standard wheelchair rear-wheel axis is typically aligned with the backrest[7] and results in a shoulder-axis position that is 2 in. in front of wheel axis[8] (Figure 4.2A), putting the patient at a biomechanical disadvantage.

Changing the position of the rear wheels relative to the seat can affect the energy requirements to self-propel, the maneuverability and stability of the wheelchair, and the weight distribution of the patient in the wheelchair (Figure 4.2B). Although patient feedback and evaluation should be conducted to determine wheel axis position, one recommendation is that the shoulder axis should be about 2 in. behind the wheel axis.[8] Another recommendation is that the wheel axis should be in line with the shoulder (or slightly forward) and the shoulder-wheel distance should be such that the elbow is in 30

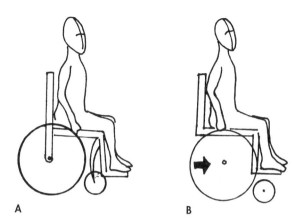

Fig. 4.2 A. In the standard wheelchair, the rear wheel axis is aligned with the backrest, pushing the patient's shoulder axis 2 in. in front of the wheel axis: Wheelchair propulsion ability may suffer. B. Wheelchair propulsion and maneuverability may improve by adjusting the rear wheel position forward relative to the patient's seat position.

degrees of flexion when the top of the handrim is grasped.[9] Research will probably be needed to determine optimal wheel position for efficient propulsion in different patient populations.

To improve self-propulsion ability, consider adjustable axial hardware to position the rear wheels in the optimal position relative to the patient's shoulder-joint axis. An active person with good trunk balance, for example, may benefit by moving the rear wheels and axis forward.[10]

Moving Rear Wheel Axis Forward[7]

- Rolls easier because weight is shifted over the rear wheel axis[10]
- Maneuverability improves if seat position is moved posteriorly relative to wheel axis (reduces moment of inertia)[8]
- Propulsion efficiency improves (i.e., recovery phase of propulsion cycle) if seat position is moved posteriorly relative to wheel axis[8]
- Easier to "pop a wheelie" for curb climbing and maneuverability if seat position is moved posterior relative to wheel axis[8]
- Reduces wheelchair's downhill turning tendency when on sloped surfaces if seat position is moved posteriorly relative to wheel axis[8]
- Shortens the wheel base
- Shortens the turning radius
- Reduces stability[8] (i.e., easier to tip backward) (Consider rear anti-tippers for patient safety.)

Moving Rear Wheel Axis Backward[10]

- Increases stability
- More energy is required to propel wheelchair
- Increases turning radius

Moving Rear Wheel Axis Upward (or Lowering Seat)[7]

- Strengthens stroke propulsion
- Increases trunk stability
- Increases buttock pressure (due to seat tilt)

Self-Feeding

Can the patient self-feed? Have the patient sit as upright as possible to facilitate hand-to-mouth skills. Even if the patient does not self-feed, try to position upright to minimize risk of aspiration. However, upright positioning may not be possible if the patient has hip extension contractures. If the patient is reclined because of limited hip flexion but needs to be more upright for safety while eating, consider a forward-tilt wheelchair. Make sure, however, that the patient is adequately supported and supervised when in a forward tilt, because forward sliding in the wheelchair is possible.

EXERCISES

1. How would you determine whether a manual, power, or attendant-operated wheelchair is most appropriate for your patient?
2. Sit at a desk with your head and trunk vertical (i.e., not leaning forward), hold a book so that you can comfortably read it, and then notice the angle of your eye gaze relative to the horizon. Note how your eyes strain if you move your eyes to look either directly straight ahead or look too far down (i.e., below 30 degrees from the horizon).
3. Sit in a wheelchair and determine how high and low you have to reach for objects on the wall (i.e., light switches), on the floor (i.e., shoes), or directly in front

of you (i.e., a door). Compare your maximal reaching ability with the recommended values for adults while reaching in a standard wheelchair.

4. What two factors should you consider to determine back support height for your patient?

5. How would moving the rear wheels forward relative to the seat affect the performance of the wheelchair and the energy requirements of your patient? How would wheelchair stability be affected?

6. How high must your patient reach to operate the buttons in an elevator?

7. What type of armrest and front rigging would you prescribe for patients performing a (a) stand-pivot transfer? (b) a sliding board transfer?

REFERENCES

1. Behrman AL. Clinical perspectives on wheelchair selection: factors in functional assessment. J Rehabil Res Dev 1990;2(suppl):17–27.

2. Miles-Tapping C, MacDonald LJ. Lifestyle implications of power mobility. Phys Occup Ther Geriatr 1994;12:31–49.

3. Kamenetz HL. The Wheelchair Book: Mobility for the Disabled. Springfield, IL: Thomas, 1969;132–134.

4. Pheasant S. Body Space: Anthropometry, Ergonomics, and Design. London: Taylor and Francis, 1996;46–67.

5. Olson SC, Meredith DK. Wheelchair Interiors. Chicago: National Easter Seal Society for Crippled Children and Adults, 1973;5–12.

6. American National Standard for Buildings and Facilities: Providing Accessibility and Usability for Physically Handicapped People. Accessible Elements and Spaces (A117.1). New York: American National Standard Institute, 1986;16–73.

7. Ragnarsson KT. Clinical perspectives on wheelchair selection: prescription considerations and a comparison of conventional and light weight wheelchairs. J Rehabil Res Dev 1990;2(suppl):8–16.

8. Brubaker C. Ergonometric considerations. J Rehabil Res Dev 1990;2(suppl):37–48.

9. Bergen AF, Presperin J, Tallman T. Positioning for Function: Wheelchairs and Other Assistive Technologies. Valhalla, NY: Valhalla Rehabilitation Publications, 1990;77.

10. Currie DM, Hardwick K, Marburger RA, Britell CW. Wheelchair Prescription and Adaptive Seating. In JL Delisa, BM Gans (eds), Rehabilitation Medicine: Principles and Practice (2nd ed). Philadelphia: Lippincott, 1993;563–585.

The Wheelchair

5

The Wheelchair: An Introduction

The wheelchair basically consists of a mobility base and a seating system (Figure 5.1). The *mobility base* (i.e., metal frame) provides the structure and mobility of the wheelchair. Mobility bases are reviewed in Chapter 6. The *seating system* is mounted to the mobility base and provides postural support for the patient. The seating system and other wheelchair components are reviewed in Chapter 7.

MOBILITY BASE

Consider the following indications, contraindication, and risks associated with using a wheelchair.

Patient Indications for a Wheelchair[1]

- Nonambulatory
- Unsafe, unsteady, or nonfunctional ambulator
- Marginal ambulator (short distances only)
- Lack of cardiopulmonary reserve
- Lower extremity (LE) weightbearing contraindicated
- Dependent LE contraindicated

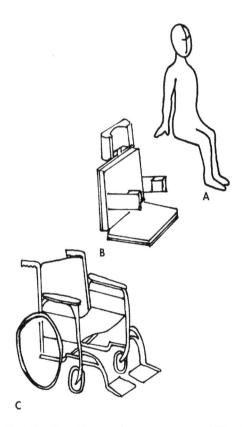

Fig. 5.1 The (A) patient, (B) postural support system, and (C) mobility base.

Possible Reasons for Using a Wheelchair

- Pain
- Weakness
- Deformity
- Loss of body part
- Incoordination
- Energy conservation[2]

Patient Contraindication for a Wheelchair

- Any condition in which sitting is contraindicated

Risks Associated with Wheelchair Use[1]

- Injury associated with unsafe mobility (e.g., falls, tips)
- Pressure sores
- Hip and knee flexion contractures
- Disuse atrophy and deconditioning
- Dependency on wheelchair

SEATING SYSTEM

The seating system provides postural support for the patient in the mobility base. *The goal is to support and safely position the patient to function maximally.* The seating system can include such wheelchair components as the seat insert, seat cushion, back insert, lateral trunk supports, hip guides, pommel, anterior trunk support, and head support. Many of the following indications could be used in the medical justification for a seating system.

General Indications for Seating Systems[3]

- Prevent deformity
- Accommodate or delay progression of an orthopedic deformity[4]
- Decrease pain
- Improve comfort[4]
- Prevent tissue damage
- Increase sitting tolerance
- Increase sitting stability
- Enhance respiratory function
- Enhance functional abilities
- Enhance mobility through positioning
- Improve body image
- Minimize influence of abnormal tone and reflexes[4]

Physical Effect of Seating Systems

- Support body parts
- Accommodate body parts and reduce pressure
- Block undesirable movements

A LITTLE THEORY

Patients who are wheelchair bound must interact with their wheelchair when solving motor problems. Because movements emerge out of the interaction between the environment and the self,[5] every possible effort should be made for the wheelchair to enhance rather than interfere with the patient's ability to perform useful movements. A lap board, for example, can provide upper extremity support. However, it can also interfere with a patient's ability to reach the rear wheels to self-propel. Try to order wheelchair bases and components that enable patients to function maximally.

EXERCISES

1. List three indications for a wheelchair.
2. Name a contraindication for wheelchair use. Is an ischial pressure sore a contradiction for sitting?
3. List five risks associated with wheelchair use.
4. List 10 possible indications for a seating system.
5. Can wheelchair components interfere with a patient's ability to function?

REFERENCES

1. Kamenetz HL. The Wheelchair Book: Mobility for the Disabled. Springfield, IL: Thomas, 1969;132–148.
2. Freney D. Pediatric seating. Home Health Care Dealer/Supplier 1995;Sept/Oct:103–105.
3. Kohlmeyer KM, Yarkony GM. Functional Outcomes After Spinal Cord Injury Rehabilitation. In GM Yarkony (ed), Spinal Cord Injury: Medical Management and Rehabilitation. Gaithersburg, MD: Aspen, 1994;9–14.
4. Taylor SJ. Evaluating the client with physical disabilities for wheelchair sitting. Am J Occup Ther 1987;41:711–716.
5. Green PH. Problems of Organization of Motor System. In R Rosen, FM Snell (eds), Progress in Theoretical Biology. San Diego: Academic, 1972;304–338.

6

The Mobility Base

A mobility base is the structural foundation of the wheelchair (the metal frame) that provides mobility for the patient. Mobility bases typically include armrests, casters, rear wheels, handrims, front rigging, wheel locks, and a sling upholstered seat and back.

Mobility base choice depends on the size, weight, strength requirements, propulsion ability, and positioning needs of the patient.

TYPE OF MOBILITY BASE

Mobility Bases to Address Manual Propulsion Ability

Standard Frame

The standard frame is the kind of wheelchair typically seen in the drugstore window and should be considered if the patient has no lower extremity (LE) range of motion limitations and has good head control. The patient will need 90 degrees of hip flexion to fit into this frame in an upright position (Figure 6.1A).

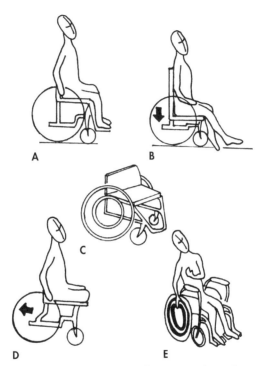

Fig. 6.1 Mobility bases that address different manual propulsion needs. A. The standard wheelchair frame requires the patient to have at least 90-degree hip flexion. B. The hemiplegic chair is lower to the ground to enable foot propulsion. C. Ultralight frames provide maneuverability and speed for the active patient with low postural needs. D. The amputee frame moves the rear wheels posteriorly to improve backward stability and to reduce the possibility of backward tipping of the wheelchair. E. The one-hand drive wheelchair allows the patient with only one functional upper extremity to self-propel using two handrims located on the same wheel.

Indications

- 90 degrees of hip flexion.
- 70-degree popliteal angles (i.e., adequate hamstring length). If knee flexion contractures are present, 90-degree front rigging may be required to support the feet.
- Functional head control.

Hemiplegic Chairs (Foot Drive)

Hemiplegic chairs should be considered if the patient needs a frame low enough to the floor to reach the ground for foot propulsion. The seat is 2 in. lower than a standard frame seat, the tires are smaller (i.e., 22-in. diameter rather than 24 in.),[1] and the front rigging is specially adapted.[1]

Patients with hemiplegia frequently use this frame. The hemiplegic frame is also useful for a short patient who needs a low seat level for transfers (Figure 6.1B).

Indications

- Foot propulsion
- Hemiplegic patients
- Transfers for short patients

Disadvantages

- Taller individuals may have difficulty standing during transfers due to the lower seat level.
- Tables may be too high while sitting in this wheelchair.

Ultralight Frames (Sports Chairs)

Ultralight frames are popular among paraplegic patients and are used in sports, such as racing and basketball, because of the wheelchair's lightweight characteristics, ease in maneuvering, and speed. Ultralight frames weigh less than a standard frame (weight ranges from 16 lb to 38 lb[1] or less[2]) but do not offer as much postural support for the trunk or LEs. Building in postural supports would, of course, make the frame heavier (Figure 6.1C).

Indications

- Activities requiring speed or quick maneuverability
- Energy-efficient propulsion (lightweight)

Advantages

- Lightweight materials (i.e., aluminum alloy, titanium, graphite)[2]
- Strong, rigid frame
- Multiple, adjustable axle position[2] to improve performance

Disadvantages

- Decreased postural and foot support
- Storage problem (if unable to fold)

Racing Wheelchair Characteristics[2]

- Rear wheels: 26–27 in.
- Narrow, high-pressure tires (160 psi)

- Small handrims: 12 in.
- Large casters with precision bearing to improve rolling performance
- Low seat: top of wheel located near the axilla; improved stability

Amputee Frame

The amputee frame positions the rear wheels at least 1 in. posteriorly to shift the center of gravity, improve the stability, and reduce the chance of the wheelchair tipping backward.[1] This frame may be considered if the patient has an amputation, if the patient places excessive body weight toward the rear of the wheelchair, or if the patient has a history of tipping wheelchairs backward (Figure 6.1D).

Indications

- LE amputations
- Low patient mass in front or high mass in rear of wheelchair
- History of backward tipping of wheelchair

Disadvantages

- Larger turning radius because frame base is longer[1]

One-Hand Drive

One-hand drive wheelchairs permit self-propulsion and steering using two wheel rims attached to only one side of the frame.[1] Pushing one rim permits the wheelchair to steer left while pushing the other rim allows the wheelchair to steer right. Pushing both rims simultaneously allows the wheelchair to go straight. The patient therefore needs to have sufficient hand function on one side to operate this mechanism. Also note that patients may tend to assume an undesirable asymmetric trunk posture by leaning to the side when operating the one-hand drive mechanism (Figure 6.1E).

Indications

- Self-propulsion using one uninvolved upper extremity (UE)
- Hemiplegic patients

Disadvantages

- Difficulty grasping and operating handrim
- Patient's tendency to assume an asymmetric posture

Mobility Bases to Address Orientation in Space

Backward Tilt-in-Space Frames

Backward tilt-in-space frames tilt backward in space like a rocking chair, except the position of the frame can be adjusted and maintained at various angles, while the hips are maintained at a fixed angle. As a result, the patient's posture can be varied from upright sitting with the patient facing front to fully tilted backward with the patient facing up toward the ceiling. This frame should be considered if patients have poor head control, poor trunk control, or tend to slide forward in the wheelchair, since gravity can assist sitting while the seat-to-back angle is kept constant (Figure 6.2A). The patient will require a head support when using this wheelchair.

Disadvantages include sensory deprivation due to the patient facing more or less toward the ceiling when the frame is tilted backwards. This frame is heavier and more costly than a standard frame. In addition, it folds into a less compact size than a standard frame by collapsing the back posts forward onto the seat.

Indications

- Poor head control
- Poor trunk control
- Forward sliding in wheelchair
- Poor tolerance for upright sitting
- Shifts weightbearing surface[3]
- Reduces reliance on anterior supports[3]
- Improves stability of head and trunk during transportation[3]

Disadvantages

- Heavier and larger than standard frame
- Folding possible but less compact
- Sensory deprivation
- Cost

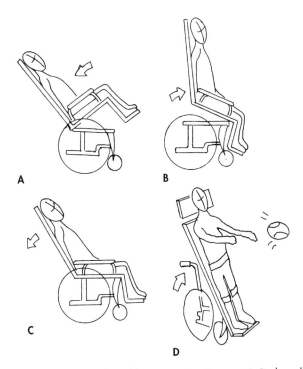

Fig. 6.2 Mobility bases that address orientation in space. A. Backward tilt-in-space frames permit gravity-assisted sitting for patients with poor sitting ability or sliding problems while the patient's hip-joint angles as well as the angle between the seat and back are kept constant. B. Forward tilt-in-space frames allow the patient to be tipped forward if a more upright position is needed. C. Reclining frames may be appropriate for patients with poor head control, poor sitting tolerance, or hip extension contractures. D. Standing mobility offers the patient interaction with the environment from a standing rather than sitting posture.

Forward Tilt-in-Space Frame

The forward tilt-in-space frame actually tilts or pitches the patient forward as if someone lifted the back legs of the chair. This frame should be considered if it is important for the patient to be upright. For example, an individual may choke if fed in a reclined position but lacks the range of motion in the hips to sit upright in a standard wheelchair. The forward tilt therefore enables the patient's body to be pitched forward as one unit. The disadvantage of this frame is that the patient tends to slide forward in the wheelchair. These frames are also costlier, heavier, and larger than a standard frame (Figure 6.2B).

Indications

- Unable to tolerate a reclined position
- LE extensor contractures

Disadvantages

- Forward sliding
- Shear associated with pelvic sliding
- Heavier and larger than standard frame
- Cost

Reclining Frame (Semi- and Full Reclining)

Reclining frames permit the back to be reclined like a lawn chair and should be considered if patients have poor head control, cannot tolerate an upright position, or have hip extension contractures. Head support is required for this frame when the patient is reclined (Figure 6.2C).

There are several disadvantages of the reclining frame. First, contact points between the patient's back and the back support of the wheelchair do not remain consistent when the back angle is changed. Instead, contact points move up cephalically as the frame reclines. As a result, patients may tend to slide forward because of shear forces created between the patient's back and the reclining back of the wheelchair.[4] Second, sensory deprivation may occur when the patient faces up toward the ceiling once the back is reclined. Third, the reclined position may facilitate undesirable extensor tone in neurologic patients due to tonic labyrinth reflex (TLR) activation.[5] Finally, reclining frames tend to be heavier and larger than standard wheelchair frames.

Indications

- If patient lacks 90 degrees of hip flexion
- Poor head control
- Poor trunk control
- Moderate trunk involvement (semireclining)[6]
- Severe trunk involvement (full reclining)[6]
- Unable to tolerate upright sitting

Disadvantages

- Shear present (Nonshear recline systems are available but are more expensive.)[4]

- Sensory deprivation (i.e., the patient faces ceiling)
- TLR may facilitate extensor tone
- Heavier and larger than standard frame

Elevating and Standing Mobility

Elevating chairs are powered and enable seat height to be raised and lowered[4] to facilitate functional reach and enhance social interaction. Standing mobility enables patients to interact from a supported standing position if sufficient LE range of motion is available (Figure 6.2D).

Indications

- Improve reach from different heights[4]
- Social interaction
- Weightbearing (standing mobility)
- Alternative positioning (standing mobility)

Disadvantages

- Any contraindications for standing (standing mobility)
- For standing mobility, sufficient hip extension, knee extension, and ankle dorsiflexion are necessary
- Cost
- Storage and portability
- Maintenance if powered
- Safety concerns related to falls from standing or elevated seating positions

Attendant-Operated Mobility Bases

Indoor Chair

Indoor chairs have large wheels in front and casters in the rear, enabling the wheelchair to be maneuvered in tight spaces.[1] Outdoor use is not recommended, because curbs and stair negotiation are difficult. Self-propulsion may also be more difficult in an indoor chair (Figure 6.3A).[1]

Indications

- Indoor use
- Small spaces

Disadvantages

- May be difficult to self-propel[1]
- Outdoor use
- Difficulty using on curbs and stairs[1]

Strollers

Strollers are a lightweight means of transportation for children and some adults who do not self-propel. The advantage of a stroller is less weight and greater portability. As a result, parents can travel around town, in stores, and on stairs with less difficulty using a stroller than using a wheelchair (Figure 6.3B).

Strollers, however, do not provide as much postural support as a wheelchair, unless support is built into the stroller (which increases weight). The big drawback of

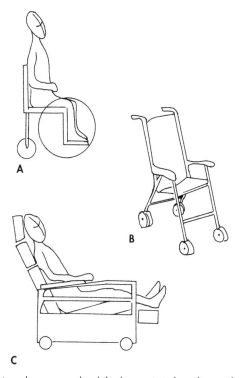

Fig. 6.3 Attendant-operated mobility bases. A. Indoor chairs, which may be difficult to self-propel, can be spotted for their larger front wheels and their ability to be maneuvered in tight indoor spaces. B. A stroller offers a lightweight, portable means of transporting a child who does not self-propel. Growth capability, postural support, and durability, however, may be less adequate in a stroller than in a wheelchair. C. Geriatric chairs offer the nonambulatory patient a padded, reclined positioning with elevating leg support for indoor use.

strollers is that the patient cannot push a stroller because the wheels are small. Growth adjustability in the stroller can also be limited. Parents may prefer a stroller to a wheelchair because they think their child looks less handicapped in the stroller. If children are capable of self-propelling a wheelchair, then placing them in a stroller will limit their independence.

Indications

- Infants
- Small children and adults who do not self-propel
- Lightweight transportation
- Accessibility in the community
- Portability
- Cosmetics (less stigma than wheelchair)

Disadvantages

- Cannot self-propel
- Less durable than a wheelchair
- Fewer postural support options
- Less growth capability

Geriatric Chairs

Geriatric chairs are mostly seen in facilities for the elderly and allow the individual to recline with feet elevated. Disadvantages include limited outdoor use, no ability to self-propel, difficult for caregiver to steer and push, difficulty to position patients, and difficulty performing two-person transfers (Figure 6.3C).

Advantages

- Head reclines and feet elevate
- Indoor use
- Padded

Disadvantages

- Cannot self-propel
- Difficulty performing two-person transfers
- Difficult for caregiver to push
- Insufficient postural support
- Not for outdoor use
- Sensory deprivation when patient is reclined

Power Mobility Bases

Power Wheelchairs (Electric Wheelchairs[7])

Power wheelchair mobility provides independence for patients who can safely operate the controls, cannot manually self-propel a wheelchair, and require postural support. Patients who are marginal manual wheelchair users may also be candidates for power mobility.[1, 4] Social, cognitive, perceptual, and functional developmental benefits using power mobility have been reported in physically disabled children as young as 24 months.[4]

The choice of mobility bases includes a standard base, a modular base, or an add-on system. Light-duty power wheelchairs are used for indoor use, whereas heavy-duty power wheelchairs are used for outdoor use and long distances (Figure 6.4A).

Type of Base
- *Standard base system*: the traditional power system, less weight than modular system.[3]
     Light-duty frames: for indoor use
     Heavy-duty frames: for outdoor and long-distance use
- *Modular base systems*: lower to ground than standard base system, sturdy, good for rugged terrain but very heavy.[3]
- *Add-on power system*: converts a manual into a power wheelchair.[3] Add-on power systems may be indicated if a manual wheelchair has been recently purchased, and there is now need for power mobility, but funding is limited. The disadvantage is that they are less durable.

Controls
Control switches can provide either graded or on-off control of a power wheelchair.[3]

- *Proportional controls* offer gradation in speed and change in direction.
- *Microswitch controls* offer on-off operation only if motor ability is limited.

Indications

- Independent mobility possible with power but not manual wheelchair.
- High quadriplegia.

A

B

Fig. 6.4   Power mobility bases. A. A standard power wheelchair is the traditional model of power mobility that offers postural support for patients who cannot self-propel a manual wheelchair. B. Scooters look like golf carts and offer power mobility for the patient with limited endurance but sufficient sitting, transfer, and upper extremity (steering) ability.

- Permanent disability[7] (i.e., not a temporary condition).
- Physical exertion is contraindicated.
- Marginal manual wheelchair user (unable to maintain appropriate rate of locomotion in manual wheelchair).[4]
- For energy conservation.[4]

Disadvantages

- Maintenance
- Cost (three times more costly than manual wheelchair)[1]
- Inaccessibility
- Need back-up manual wheelchair[8]
- Lacks portability, folding, and storage

Motorized Carts (Scooters)

Patients using a motorized cart or scooter (looks like a golf cart) generally require better sitting ability, transfer ability, and manual upper limb (steering wheel) ability than do patients using a power wheelchair. Patients may be marginal ambulators.[1,4] Scooters are lighter and narrower than power wheelchairs. In addition, there may be less of a stigma attached to a cart than a power wheelchair.[1] Be cautious about recommending a scooter to a patient who has a progressive disability and may soon lack the transfer, UE function, or postural support to use a scooter. In this case, a power wheelchair may be more appropriate.[8] Scooter selection is based in part on whether it will be used indoors, outdoors, or both indoors and outdoors* (Figure 6.4B).

---

*Personal communication. CM Rivette. Amigo Mobility Intl., Inc. October 3, 1997.

Indications

- Marginal ambulator
- Patients with limited stamina[8]
- Requires good transfer skills, sitting balance, and UE function

Advantages[3]

- Lighter in weight than a power wheelchair
- Narrower than a power wheelchair
- Looks less handicapping than a power wheelchair

Disadvantages

- Maintenance
- Cost
- Inaccessibility
- Lacks portability, folding, and storage
- Lacks postural support
- Stability problems (incidence of tipping over)

Both power wheelchairs and carts require routine *battery charging*. Power wheelchairs and carts do not fair well in *poorly accessible neighborhoods* where curb cuts, ramps, and beveled sidewalks are absent. Both are heavier than manual wheelchairs, which makes getting up one step with assistance difficult and getting up more than one step close to impossible. In addition, if a power wheelchair or scooter breaks down, it is much heavier to push home than the manual wheelchair. (It is a little like pushing a car in neutral gear as compared with pushing a bicycle.)

Consider a manual wheelchair as a back-up in case the power wheelchair breaks down.

The Future?

Who knows what the future generation of wheelchairs will look like? I envision a chair that would be able to elevate (i.e., like a barber's chair), spin around (i.e., like an office chair), and tilt in any direction.

SIZE

What Size Should the Frame Be?

The size of the wheelchair is determined, of course, by the size of the patient (see Chapter 3). Record the patient's seat width, seat depth, back height, and heel-to-knee measurement.* [1] Be aware that frame size names and dimensions may vary among manufacturers. This list, however, should give you a starting point when communicating with dealers:

- *Preschool size*[1]: 10-in. seat width and 8-in. seat depth
- *Pediatric size**: 12- or 14-in. seat width and 11.5-in. seat depth
- *Junior size*[1]: 16-in. seat width and 14-in. seat depth
- *Narrow adult size**: 16-in. seat width and 16-in. seat depth
- *Adult size*[1]: 18-in. seat width and 16-in. seat depth

---

*Personal communication. M Nassie. Quickie Designs, Inc. September 8, 1997.

- *Wide adult size*[1,9]: 20- to 28-in. seat width and 16-in. seat depth

Typical Dimensions for an Adult-Size Wheelchair

A standard, adult-size wheelchair has an outside width a little more than 2 ft and a 4-ft length. Push handles are 3 ft from the floor, and the seat is a little more than 1.5 ft from the floor.[10] Typical adult-size wheelchair dimensions are the following[10]:

- Outside width in front: 18 in.
- Outside width in rear: 26 in.
- Length of wheelchair: 48 in.
- Push handles: 36 in. from the floor
- Armrests: 30 in. from the floor
- Seat: 19 in. from the floor

Wheelchair Width

Standard wheelchair outside width is 26 in.[10] Avoid making the wheelchair wider than absolutely necessary, because the patient's wheelchair may not pass through the front door of his or her home or fit onto a van or bus ramp. Narrowing devices, which use a gear and crank mechanism, have been used on frames to temporarily narrow the wheelchair width a few inches for clearance.[1]

On the other hand, if the wheelchair is too narrow, the frame may be too unstable and the patient could tip over sideways. If this is the case, consider angling the rear wheels (camber) or obtaining a wider frame to improve stability.

Wide Wheelchairs

- Problems fitting through doorways
- Problems on van or bus ramps
- Less postural stability and increased risk of scoliosis if no postural supports on wheelchair[9]
- Problems reaching rear wheels and handrims to self-propel

STRENGTH AND CONSTRUCTION

How strong should the frame be? The strength of the frame depends on the patient's activity level, patient's body weight, and the terrain. Determine if a heavy-duty, lightweight, or standard construction is necessary.

Heavy-Duty Frame

Heavy-duty frames should be considered for patients who are heavy, exhibit very strong extensor activity, or propel under rugged terrain conditions. These frames can have reinforced joints, double cross-braces, and steel construction.

Indications

- Heavy patients
- Strong extensor tone or activity
- Patient breaks wheelchair parts
- Rough, outdoor terrain

Disadvantages

- Increased weight

- Cost

Lightweight Frame

Lightweight frames use lighter weight materials.[11]

Indications

- Negotiating inclines[12]
- Need to load wheelchair in and out of the car by hand[12]
- No elevators (The caregiver must carry wheelchair up stairs.)
- Easier for some caregivers to push wheelchair
- Improve mechanical efficiency of self-propelling patient (may have little effect on level surfaces[12])

Disadvantages

- Susceptible to greater wear and tear than standard frame
- Frame may break under heavy use

Standard Frame Construction

Indication

- General use for patient- or caregiver-assisted wheelchair propulsion

PORTABILITY

Wheelchairs that fold and have removable components can be more easily stored during transportation. Wheelchairs may fold toward the middle like an accordion, fold forward on themselves like a suitcase, or not fold at all.

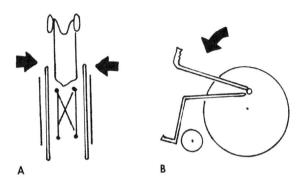

Fig. 6.5 A. Standard frames fold toward the middle like an accordion.
B. A tilt-in-space frame folds forward onto itself.

Folding Versus Nonfolding Frames

- Nonfolding frames are generally more durable than folding frames.
- Folding frames can be stored and transported in small spaces. Standard frames fold toward the middle like an accordion (Figure 6.5A). The back posts of a tilt-in-space frame, on the other hand, fold forward like a suitcase (Figure 6.5B).

Detachable Wheelchair Components

Wheelchairs can also be made lighter and more portable during transportation by removing components from the frame. Consider ordering removable features such as the following:

- Quick-release rear wheels
- Removable seat and back inserts
- Removable head supports
- Detachable front rigging
- Removable armrests

OTHER ISSUES TO CONSIDER

Like people, wheelchairs have weight, height, and an appearance.

Wheelchair Weight

The rule is, the more components the wheelchair has, the heavier it is. A heavier wheelchair often means more effort when starting and stopping. You can gain a greater appreciation of how much a wheelchair weighs by pushing it around all day than by reading 100 engineer reports on weight specifications. It is a lot of work. Do not take away the patient's function by making the wheelchair too heavy.

Height of Wheelchair

The standard seat height is 19 in. from the floor. A cushion can raise the seat height. Taller patients often need a higher seat position. However, if the wheelchair seat is too high, it may be difficult for caregivers to see where they are going when pushing the wheelchair from behind. These wheelchairs may also require a higher van roof for head clearance during transportation. Finally, a higher seat height may be less stable for patients. Be aware of the effect of seat height for knee clearance under tables and two-person transfers.

High Wheelchair Seat Problems

- Higher center of gravity and less stability
- Difficult for short caregivers to see ahead while pushing wheelchair
- Head level may be too high for clearance on low-roof vans
- Difficulty reaching floor for foot-assisted propulsion
- Difficult for two-person assisted transfers (lifting)
- Knee level may be too high for clearance under a table
- Transfers may be more difficult for short patients

Shorter patients often need a lower seat height. If the wheelchair or seat is too low, tall caregivers may strain to push the wheelchair. This is also true if the wheelchair tilts backward, which lowers the push-handle position toward the floor. Stroller handle attachments may be ordered to raise the position of the push handles.

Low Wheelchair Seat Problems

- Tall caregivers may strain to push the wheelchair.
- Front rigging may drag on ground if lowered to accommodate patient's leg length.
- Table level may be too high.
- Transfers may be difficult for tall patients.

How High Should the Push Handles Be?

The push-handle height of a standard adult wheelchair is 3 ft from the floor. To determine optimal pushing height for a particular caregiver, calculate 70–80% of the caregiver's floor-to-shoulder height.[13] For example, if the floor-to-shoulder height of a caregiver measures 40 in., then the push-handle height would be 70% of 40 in., or 28 in. from the floor (i.e., $40 \times 0.70 = 28$ in.). Determine if this calculated height is a comfortable push-handle height for the caregiver and if the dealer can order push handles close to that height. Alternatively, you may simply ask the caregiver what push-handle height would be comfortable for pushing the wheelchair.

Appearance

Since client tastes and self-image are factors in wheelchair selection,[14] it is always a good idea to show a picture of the wheelchair if it is not possible to bring in the actual wheelchair model that is to be recommended to the patient and family. That way, no one is in shock when the wheelchair is delivered.

Safety Issues

Fire Retardance

All upholstery should be fire retardant, because smoking-related fatalities have been reported in wheelchair users.[15]

Tie-Down Systems

All mobility bases must be secured by the frame to the floor of a bus using four approved straps.

EXERCISES

1. What would be the rationale (i.e., indicators) for ordering the following mobility bases?
   a. Standard
   b. Foot drive
   c. Ultralight
   d. Amputee frame
   e. One-hand drive
   f. Backward tilt-in-space
   g. Forward tilt-in-space
   h. Standing frame
   i. Indoor chair
   j. Geriatric chair
   k. Stroller
   l. Standard power wheelchair (light-duty)
   m. Standard power wheelchair (heavy-duty)
   n. Motorized cart (scooter)
2. A patient has multiple sclerosis, is nonambulatory, and is being evaluated for power mobility. He or she is currently having increasing difficulty transferring and sitting without assistance. What would you prescribe for this patient?

REFERENCES

1. Wilson AB, McFarland SR. Types of wheelchairs. J Rehabil Res Dev 1990;2(suppl):104–116.
2. Ragnarsson KT. Clinical perspectives on wheelchair selection: prescription considerations and a comparison of conventional and light weight wheelchairs. J Rehabil Res Dev 1990;2(suppl):8–16.
3. Harrymann SE, Warren LR. Positioning and Power Mobility. In G Church, S Glennen (eds), The Handbook of Assistive Technologies. San Diego: Singular, 1992;55–92.
4. Warren CG. Technical considerations: power mobility and its implications. J Rehabil Res Dev 1990;2(suppl):44–85.
5. Fiorentino MR. Reflex Testing Methods for Evaluating CNS Development (2nd ed). Springfield, IL: Thomas, 1981;17.
6. Delisa JA, Greenberg S. Wheelchair prescription guidelines. Am Fam Physician 1982;24:145–150.
7. Miles-Tapping C, MacDonald LJ. Lifestyle implications of power mobility. Phys Occup Ther Geriatr 1994;12:31–49.
8. Currie DM, Hardwick K, Marburger RA, Britell CW. Wheelchair Prescription and Adaptive Seating. In JL Delisa, BM Gans (eds), Rehabilitation Medicine: Principles and Practice (2nd ed). Philadelphia: Lippincott, 1993;563–585.
9. Kamenetz HL. The Wheelchair Book: Mobility for the Disabled. Springfield, IL: Thomas, 1969;128–134.
10. American National Standard for Buildings and Facilities: Providing Accessibility and Usability for Physically Handicapped People. Accessible Elements and Spaces (A117.1). New York: American National Standard Institute, 1986;16–73.
11. Mattingly D. Wheelchair selection. Orthop Nurs 1993;12:11–17.
12. Brubaker C. Ergonometric considerations. J Rehabil Res Dev 1990;2(suppl):37–48.
13. Pheasant S. Body Space: Anthropometry, Ergonomics, and Design. London: Taylor and Francis, 1996;132.
14. Taylor SJ. Evaluating the client with physical disabilities for wheelchair sitting. Am J Occup Ther 1987;41:711–716.
15. Calder CJ, Kirby RL. Fatal wheelchair-related accidents in the United States. Am J Phys Med Rehabil 1990;69:184–190.

7

Seating System and Wheelchair Components

Shopping for wheelchair components is a little like buying suits: They can be bought commercially (from the shelf) or custom made (made to fit). When possible, consider less costly commercially available parts that can sufficiently address the patient's needs. The most common wheelchair components, including seating system components, are reviewed in this chapter. Note: Alternative terminology is in parentheses.

COMMERCIAL VERSUS CUSTOM-MADE COMPONENTS

Commercially available components are

- Available
- Less costly
- Less tailored to specific needs

Custom-made components are

- Specific to patient's special needs
- More costly

- Not as readily available as they take longer to fabricate

HEADREST (HEAD SUPPORTS)[1]

The headrest is a support structure located behind the patient's head on the wheelchair (Figure 7.1).

Indications

- Difficulty maintaining head upright
- Support for the head while in a reclined or backward tilt position[2]
- May help protect against whiplash injury during bus or van transportation

Disadvantages

- May interfere with two-person transfers (Consider removable headrests.)
- Adds weight to the wheelchair

Types

Head support shapes are planar (flat) or curved depending on how much contact is needed between the patient's head and the headrest.

Comments

- Consider a *planar headrest* if the patient needs support primarily behind the head.

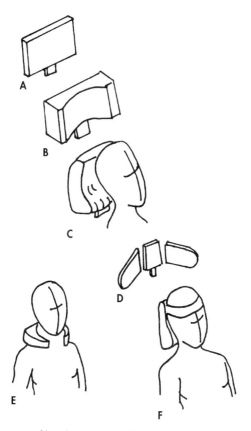

Fig. 7.1 Types of head supports. A. Planar. B. Curved. C. Curved headrest with occipital support. D. Central and side panels. E. Neck ring. F. Head band.

- Consider a *curved headrest* if the patient needs lateral support for the head (i.e., head falls to the side). Side panels can provide additional lateral support.
- Consider *occipital support or ledge* (i.e., where the neck and back of the head meet), if the patient has a shelf-like curve or shape in this area of the head. The ledge, which can be built into the shape of the headrest, can provide added points of contact and support for the patient's head. Although the ledge can provide cervical support in flexion, some patients may respond with undesirable scapula elevation and extensor tone.[3]
- Headrests can affect head position, muscle tone, neck position, and swallowing ability.[4]
- If the patient has strong extensor tone or activity, consider a reinforced, stronger headrest system.
- If the patient tends to hook his or her head around the side of the headrest, consider a wider headrest or deep headrest with lateral walls (side panels) to block the hooking movement.
- If the headrest is too high (i.e., above the crown of the head), it may block the vision of the attendant who pushes the wheelchair and may interfere with clearance through low-roof vans.
- If the headrest is too wide (i.e., in excess of ear-to-ear width), it may block the patient's view behind the wheelchair.
- If the side panels of a headrest are too narrow (i.e., less than ear-to-ear width), irritation of the ears, temporal

mandibular joint, or the lateral corner of the eye may result from friction and rubbing.

- *Neck rings* or *collars* (i.e., cervical supports attached to wheelchair) may help maintain the patient's head in an erect position[5] and keep his or her neck centered.[3]
- *Head bands* (i.e., bands attached to the headrest that provide anterior support around the patient's forehead) have been used to position the patient's head back into the postural support structure.[3] Head bands and other head-support structures have been used by some patients who lack head control but need to function from an upright position.
- *Caution is required for any devices used around the head.* Items used around the patient's head and neck should be evaluated carefully and supervised adequately due to risk of injury. Patients who slide forward in their wheelchair or are poorly positioned can become caught on these devices. Furthermore, devices around the head can affect tone, swallowing, and posture.[4]
- Try to provide the least restrictive environment with the minimal amount of components to achieve the goals of sitting. One strategy is to provide gravity-assisted support (tilt-in-space or reclining wheelchair) to minimize the patient's reliance on anterior head and trunk supports.

BACK INSERTS

A back insert is a back-support structure on the wheelchair.

Indications

- Back inserts provide postural support for the patient's spine and trunk.

Types

Types of back supports include sling back, planar, contoured, and custom molded (Figure 7.2). Back insert shapes are planar, contoured (curved), or custom molded depending on how much insert shape is needed to maximize contact of the patient's back with the insert. The more severe a fixed deformity or asymmetry, the greater the need for custom-molded support (Figure 7.3).

Sling-Back Upholstery

Sling-back upholstery provides a backrest that is usually made of vinyl material and attached to the back rails of the frame. This type of backrest offers minimal postural support and can cause a hammock or rounding effect on the patient's back, giving the patient a fetal-like appearance.

Planar or Linear Inserts

Planar or linear inserts are flat support structures that provide midline stability in mildly involved patients.[4]

Indications

- Minimal orthopedic problems
- Sitting range of motion is within normal limits
- Able to assume upright sitting

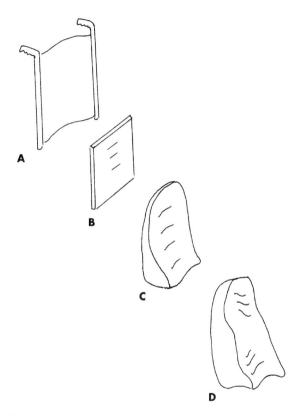

Fig. 7.2   Back supports from least to most support include (A) sling back, (B) planar, (C) contoured, and (D) custom molded.

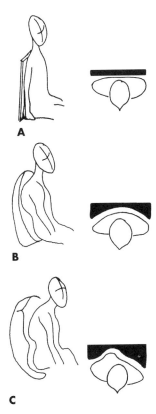

Fig. 7.3 A. Planar back inserts provide support for mildly involved patients with minimal orthopedic problems. B. Contoured back inserts provide support and accommodate deformity in moderately involved patients. C. Custom-contoured back inserts (molded) provide accommodating support for severely involved patients with fixed, asymmetric deformity.

Planar Combined with Contoured Inserts

Combining contoured and planar support structures may help correct and accommodate patient deformities in moderately involved patients.[4]

<u>Indications</u>

- Moderate tone and strength problems
- Moderate orthopedic problems
- Less than 30-degree scoliosis
- Unable to assume symmetric sitting

Custom-Contoured Seating

Custom-contoured (molded) seats are curved support structures to accommodate deformity in the severely involved patient.[4] Note that contoured backs can provide a tight fit and may interfere with weight shifting and postural adjustments, as well as upper extremity (UE) movements in patients who have those abilities.

<u>Indications</u>

- Severe tone
- Severe bony deformity
- Altered sensation

Disadvantages of Back Inserts

- The back insert may position the patient too far forward in the wheelchair, making reach for wheels during propulsion more difficult.[2] Consider adjustable rear wheel axles to move wheels forward and closer to the upper limbs or consider hardware to move the back insert further to the rear of the frame.

- Weight is added to the wheelchair.
- Folding of the wheelchair is more difficult. The back insert must be removed before folding the wheelchair. Sling-type supports do not have this problem.

Comments

- Patients who sit well using only the sling-back uphol-stery on the wheelchair may not require an insert.
- Patients with "relatively" flat backs may benefit from a flat (planar) insert. Some clinicians, however, argue that because the healthy back exhibits a mild lumbar arch, the back insert should follow the contour of the back to provide more than just planar support.
- Patients with fixed, rounded backs, such as geriatric patients with kyphosis, may benefit more from curved (spoon-shaped) back inserts.
- Patients with a severely fixed curvature of the back (scoliosis) may benefit from a custom-molded insert.[4] The molded insert should be a mirror copy of the back, fitting the patient like a glove and accommo-dating the hollow and hump like shape of the patient's back. Because a molded insert is cast like a crown for a tooth, it cannot be modified later. There-fore, a molded insert is not recommended if the patient's weight or body shape is likely to change.

Note that clinicians and dealers need to have experience to produce a good mold.[6]

- The back angle may be reclined 2–5 degrees from the vertical,[7] because the patient may feel as if he or she is falling forward if he or she sits with the back insert absolutely vertical.
- Back height is determined by the sitting balance requirements and activity level of the patient.[8] A higher back provides more spinal support but may also limit trunk mobility. A lower back provides less spinal support and may increase risk of spinal deformity, but facilitates the ability to "pop a wheelie."[7] The lumbar spine needs to be supported regardless of back height.[9]
- If a high back height (i.e., above the inferior angle of the scapula level) is required, consider rounding the top edges of the back insert to permit scapula mobility for less restricted, manual self-propulsion.[7]

SEAT INSERTS AND CUSHIONS

A seat insert is a seat support structure usually consisting of a base (i.e., wood, metal, or plastic) and cushion.

Indications

- Seat inserts:
    Provide support for patient's pelvis, hips, and thighs
    Can discourage a hammock effect, which gives the
        patient a fetal-like appearance in the wheelchair

- Seat cushions:
    Offer comfort
    Reduce pressure
    Distribute body weight

Types of Seat Inserts

Seat inserts are planar (flat), curved, or custom molded, depending on how much contact, support, and pressure distribution is needed between the patient and the seat (Figure 7.4). Sling-seat upholstery provides poor postural support and promotes a hammock effect, resulting in hip adduction, internal rotation, and a fetal-like posture in the patient.

- Planar inserts: for patients with no deformity.
- Curved or modular inserts: for patients with rounded surfaces who require more contact and pressure distribution.
- Custom-molded or contoured inserts: for the patient with fixed deformity (e.g., pelvis obliquity, windswept deformity). Molded inserts distribute pressure well, but may restrict transfer activities and limit weight-shifting ability.[10]

Local Shape of Seat Inserts

See Figure 7.5. The seat may be shaped to address patients' special needs, including

- *Undercut*: Front edge of the seat is beveled to clear tight hamstring tendons.
- *Antithrust seat*: The seat surface is sloped to discourage forward sliding.

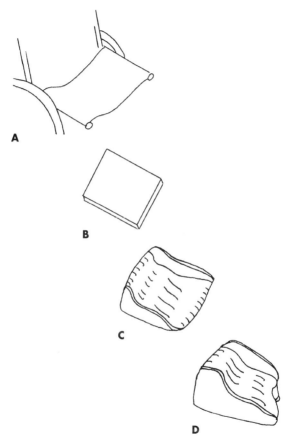

Fig. 7.4 Seat supports can be (A) sling, (B) planar, (C) curved, or (D) custom molded. Sling seating provides poor postural support.

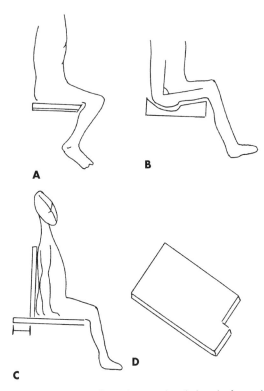

Fig. 7.5 A. Seat inserts can be undercut or beveled on the front edge for patients with knee flexion contractures to provide additional clearance of tight hamstring tendons. B. Antithrust seats help discourage forward sliding in the wheelchair for patients with adequate hip flexion. C. Growth tails are extra seat material in the rear of the insert that can be used in the future to accommodate patient growth. D. Split seats accommodate and support the thighs of patients with leg length discrepancies.

- *Growth tail*: Additional seat material is hidden behind the back insert, which can be used to increase seat depth as the patient grows.
- *Split seat insert*: Front of the seat is cut back to accommodate a leg length discrepancy.

Disadvantages of Seat Inserts

- Seat inserts raise the height of the seat, resulting in potentially greater problems transferring, a higher center of gravity, a longer reach to the rear wheels for self-propulsion, and reduced knee clearance under tables. Consider a hemiframe or hardware to lower the seat insert position to facilitate transfer. Consider adjustable rear wheel axles to move the wheels up and closer to the hands to facilitate self-propulsion.
- Weight is added to the wheelchair.
- Folding of the wheelchair is more difficult (i.e., insert must first be removed).
- Aggressively curved seat inserts (i.e., antithrust seats) can interfere with the patient's ability to transfer out of the wheelchair.

Types of Wheelchair Cushions

Seat cushions are generally classified as using air, gel or flotation, or foam materials and function to provide comfort and pressure reduction. Each technology has its advantages and disadvantages.

Static Seat Cushions[9, 11]

Air-filled
- Lightweight
- Easy to clean
- Compartmentalized
- Difficult to use in transfers
- Unstable
- Subject to puncture
- Requires monitoring of pressure level

Gel or Flotation
- Gel, water, or chemically filled
- Easy to clean
- Gels may simulate body fat[10]
- Adjust to body movements[10]
- Heavy
- May leak
- May be difficult to use during transfers
- User may develop an intolerance for other cushion types[10]

Foam (Polyurethane)
- Lightweight
- Less expensive
- Cut to size
- Wide variety[10]
- Easy to use during transfer
- Stable base
- Readily available

- Breathable[10]
- Difficult to clean
- May wear within 6 months
- May lose support and pressure-relief properties[10]
- May not be choice for long-term use
- Deteriorates with sun exposure
- Affected by temperature

Combination of Materials (Hybrids)
Combining materials (e.g., gels, air, foam) can provide properties best suited for a particular patient.[10] For example, the use of multiple layers of foam with different densities can be combined to achieve the desired level of support and comfort characteristics for a patient.

Dynamic Seating

Dynamic seating uses mechanical means requiring an external power source for changing pressure areas under the user in the seat. Disadvantages include added weight, limited mobility, and reliance on an external power source.[10]

Inappropriate Seat Dimensions

- *If the seat is too deep*, the front of the seat may press into the back of the knee and cause the patient to slide forward in the wheelchair (Figure 7.6A). In my opinion, excessive seat depth is one of the most common errors when fitting a wheelchair to a patient and a frequent reason for sacral sitting.

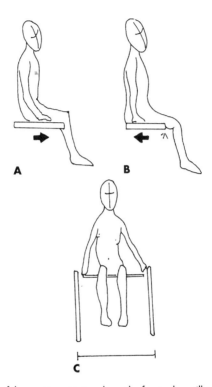

Fig. 7.6 A. If the seat insert is too deep, the front edge will press against the back of the knee and cause pressure, resulting in poor positioning with sacral sitting. Excessive seat depth is a very common error when fitting a wheelchair for a patient. B. A short seat depth results in inadequate thigh support, excessive pressure under the distal posterior thigh, and the potential for forward sitting in the wheelchair. C. A wide seat may result in difficulty self-propelling and inadequate postural support.

- *If the seat is too short*, the patient may not have enough support under the thigh and he or she may slide forward in the wheelchair (Figure 7.6B). (Think of how unstable it is to sit on a bicycle seat.) There should be no more than 2 in. of space between the back of the knee and the front edge of the seat once the patient is properly positioned to the rear of the seat.
- *If the seat is too wide*, the wheelchair may also be too wide (Figure 7.6C). The patient may have difficulty reaching the rear wheels for self-propulsion[2] and may be at a greater risk of developing scoliosis.[2] In general, seat width should be no more that 2 in. wider than the patient's hip-to-hip measurement.
- *If the seat is too high* (thick), it may raise the patient too high from the floor, making transfers into the wheelchair difficult. Short patients generally need a low seat, whereas taller patients require a higher seat.[2]
- *If the seat is too low*, the patient may be too low when working at table surfaces.

Comments

- *There is no single best seat cushion for all patients*.[12] Multiple factors, including pressure-reducing properties, stability, ease in transfers, level of maintenance, weight, and wear, need to be considered. Each patient should be individually evaluated with a variety of cushions.[10] I am not aware of any static cushion that guarantees to prevent a pressure sore from developing.

- *Materials for reducing pressure.* Pressure reduction can come in the form of solids, liquids, and gases. If the patient is not at risk for skin breakdown, foam material (solid) may be sufficient for comfort. If the patient is at risk for skin breakdown, gel, water (liquids), air (gas), or solid (foam) cushions need to be evaluated to determine the best pressure-reducing cushion for that particular patient.

- *Pressure-measuring devices can be helpful* in selecting a cushion for a particular patient if the device is reliable and valid. Studies may also provide some useful information in selecting a cushion if the patient population under study is relevant, sample size is sufficient, procedures are consistent, measuring instruments are valid, statistical analysis is appropriate, and data are interpreted correctly.

- *Choose a cushion together with the wheelchair.*[13] The fit of the patient will be affected by both the cushion and frame. Evaluate and order both at the same time if possible.

- *Avoid donut-type cushions* as they may cause venous congestion and predispose the patient to pressure sores.[14]

- *Seat angle can be inclined 1–4 degrees* above the horizon (front edge slightly higher than back edge) to help maintain the patient's position in the wheelchair.[7]

- *If the patient is a child*, make sure there is extra seat material toward the rear of the wheelchair (i.e., growth tail) that can be used as the patient grows.

- *If the patient has knee flexion contractures* or if the patient propels with the feet, consider beveling the front of the seat to allow for adequate clearance behind the knee.

- *If the patient tends to slide forward* but has full hip flexion range of motion, consider an antithrust seat. Sitting in an antithrust seat is a little like sitting in a bucket. The buttock sinks down into a trough and makes it difficult to slide out.

LATERAL TRUNK SUPPORTS

Lateral trunk supports (lateral thoracic supports[1]) are side-support structures for the patient's trunk (Figure 7.7).

Purpose

- Provide side support for the trunk
- Act as a tactile reminder to sit upright

Indications

- Patients with poor or fair trunk balance
- Patients who fall to the side[15]
- Patients with scoliosis[15]

Disadvantages

- Brachial plexus injuries can occur if lateral supports press into axilla (Figure 7.7C).
- Reduced space is available for thick (i.e., winter) clothing.
- Supports may restrict arm movements (i.e., propulsion, reaching).
- Patient may rely on external support rather than the use of his or her own muscles to sit upright

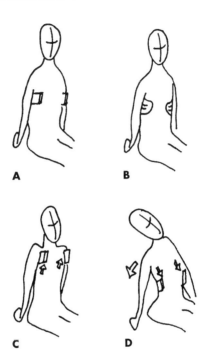

Fig. 7.7 A. Planar lateral supports provide trunk support in the coronal plane. B. Contoured lateral supports offer greater pressure distribution. C. Lateral trunk supports that press into the axilla can cause neurovascular problems. D. Lateral trunk supports that are too low offer inadequate coronal support.

Types

Lateral trunk support shape can be *planar* or *contoured* (curved) around the sides of the trunk.

- *Planar*: provides flat, padded support (Figure 7.7A)
- *Contoured* (curved): provides more contact and pressure distribution over the rounded trunk surfaces, but can make it more difficult for patients to transfer because the supports curve around the sides of the trunk (Figure 7.7B)
- *Swing-away hardware*: allows lateral trunk supports to swing out of the way to facilitate transfers or while the patient is reclined in a wheelchair

Comments

- If you are using a reclining frame, seriously consider using swing-away lateral trunk supports so that the lateral supports do not ride up into the axilla of the patient as the backrest is reclined.
- If lateral trunk supports are positioned *too far apart* so that they do not physically contact the sides of the patient, they may not function effectively to support the trunk in an upright position.
- If lateral trunk supports are positioned *too close together* (i.e., less than the patient's chest width), they can cause excessive pressure into the sides of the chest, interfere with breathing, restrict trunk movements, and cause pressure sores.

- If lateral trunk supports are positioned *too high into the axilla*, they can cause excessive pressure, circulatory compromise, and nerve injuries to the brachial plexus.
- If lateral trunk supports are positioned *too low* (i.e., below the costal level), they may not function effectively to support the trunk in midline (Figure 7.7D).
- If lateral trunk supports are *too thick*, they may interfere with arm movements. Consider making the laterals as thin as possible (i.e., 1 in. in thickness or less).
- Gravity-assisted backward tilt may improve tolerance for lateral supports in patients with scoliosis.[4]

ANTERIOR TRUNK SUPPORTS

Anterior trunk supports[1] provide support for the front of the patient's trunk area, over each shoulder, or both (Figure 7.8). The patient with poor sitting balance whose trunk lists forward may need anterior trunk support.

Indications

- Prevents the trunk and shoulders from falling forward[4]
- May assist in keeping the shoulders back
- May provide stability if shoulders elevate[4]

Disadvantages

- Safety issue of strangulation if patient slides forward, resulting in the anterior trunk support riding up to the neck[16, 17]

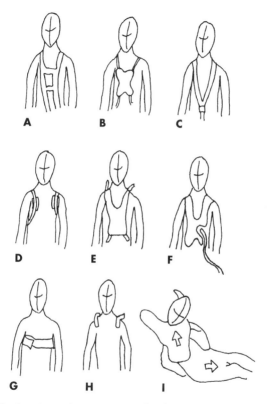

Fig. 7.8 Anterior trunk supports. A. H chest harness. B. Butterfly harness. C. V chest harness. D. Shoulder harness. E. Vest harness. F. Custom harness. G. Chest strap. H. Shoulder retractors. I. Strangulation can occur if the anterior trunk support is improperly donned or the patient slides forward in the wheelchair.

- May interfere with ability to reach and breathe if the trunk support is too tightly secured

Types

Although there are many anterior trunk support styles, their unique advantages are not always evident. In my opinion, many of these supports are useful in keeping the trunk from falling completely forward but may not markedly improve postural alignment. Consider gravity-assisted positioning using tilt or reclining frames to minimize reliance on trunk supports, improve trunk alignment, and reduce the risk of harness-related injuries (i.e., strangulation). Shoulder harnesses and retractors act on the shoulders to indirectly provide anterior trunk support.

- *H chest harness* is shaped like the letter H (Figure 7.8A).
- *Butterfly harness* is shaped like a butterfly (Figure 7.8B).
- *V chest harness* is shaped like a letter V. Straps provide greater clearance under the neck but may cut into the sides of the patient's neck if not padded (Figure 7.8C).
- *Shoulder harness* provides a posterior force for each shoulder, like a backpack, but may interfere with the forward reaching ability of the patient (Figure 7.8D). In my experience, a shoulder harness helps postural alignment in patients with (flexible) kyphosis.
- *Vest harness* provides maximal contact with trunk (Figure 7.8E).
- *Custom harness* is traced to the shape of the patient with deformity or special needs (Figure 7.8F).

- *Chest straps* (belts) secure across the patient's chest, rather than over the shoulders, as is the case with a chest harness. Chest straps may offer gentle support to sit upright.[4] Chest straps permit shoulder movements but are not as effective as other anterior trunk supports in keeping shoulders back (Figure 7.8G).
- *Shoulder retractors* are padded, rigid supports that hook over each shoulder and help prevent the shoulders and trunk from listing forward. These devices severely restrict trunk mobility, can interfere with UE mobility, and may not be tolerated by all patients (Figure 7.8H).

Comments

- Make sure the anterior trunk support is not positioned close to the patient's neck to reduce the risk of strangulation (Figure 7.8I).[17]
- Make sure the anterior trunk support does not press against and occlude gastrointestinal tubes or other lines exiting the patient's abdominal or chest wall.
- Make sure the patient's shoulders are sufficiently broad on each side, so that the shoulder-strap portion of the support can drape over the shoulder. Some patients have a very narrow area between the neck and shoulder, thus offering only a small purchase area for the strap to rest. If this is the case, consider a chest strap.

- The anterior trunk support (harness) should not be secured with the seat belt. Instead, use four separate straps to secure the anterior support.
- When donning the anterior support (harness), the bottom two straps should be secured and tightened before the top two straps are adjusted to avoid having the support ride up into the patient's neck area.

ARMRESTS

The armrests[8] (arm supports[1]), located on each side of the mobility base, are support structures for the UEs.

Indications

- Support UE[2]
- Assist in weight shifting and pressure reduction[2]
- Provide support during transfers
- Protect clothes from elements and dirt if side panels are included[7]

Types of Armrest Features[13, 18]

- *No armrests*: patient has no UE support but has good access to wheels for propulsion and sliding board transfers.
- *Fixed*: nonremovable and durable but may interfere with transfers.
- *Removable*: facilitates sliding board and two-person assisted transfers. Removable armrests add width to wheelchair (i.e., about 2 in.).[2]

- *Tubular, padded*: not strong but greater access to rear wheels (Figure 7.9A).[3]
- *Desk length*: provides access to a desk area but may offer inadequate UE support (Figure 7.9B).
- *Full length*: assists UE in transfers, provides support for patients with lordoses and obesity,[2] and supports lap board use but limits access to desk areas (Figure 7.9C).
- *Adjustable height*: to optimize height for UE support, transfers, lap-tray level, and growth in children.[3]
- *Double posted*: stronger than single-posted arms but more difficult to remove (see Figure 7.9C).
- *Single posted*: provides UE support, easy to remove, but not durable (Figure 7.9D).
- *Double length*: provides sideways protection for reclining frames.[3] Longer lengths may also be available.
- *Wraparound*[9]: reduces frame width.

Comments

If Armrests Too Low

- Poor posture (slumped)
- Increased fatigue
- Respiration can be affected

If Armrests Too High

- Elevated scapula
- Interferes with handrim reach for self-propulsion

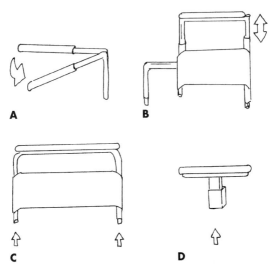

Fig. 7.9 Types of armrest features. A. Tubular arms can swing away and allow greater access to handrims. B. Desk-length arms enable closer access under tables. Adjustable height arms enable up or down arm pad position to properly support the upper extremities, facilitate pressure-relief weight shifts, and allow upper extremity push-off during transfers. C. Full-length arms provide greater length to facilitate push-off during stand-pivot transfers and offer a supportive surface for a lap board. A double-posted armrest provides a durable base for patients who tend to break equipment. D. Armrests with single posting enable easier removal of armrests.

CLOTHES GUARD

A clothes guard[18] (skirt guard) is located on the sides of the wheelchair seat near armrests to protect the user from wheel debris.

LAP BOARD

A lap board[1] (lap tray, UE support surface[3]) is a rigid, flat board secured over the armrests (see Chapter 1; Figure 1.1). Lap boards provide a table surface for eating, school work, communication devices, and greater UE support while the patient is in the wheelchair. The lap board may interfere with independent transfer ability.

Indications

- Provides a work area on the wheelchair instead of using a desk[2,19]
- Provides support surface for feeding[19]
- Provides surface for communication boards[19]
- Provides a surface to mount sensors for power wheelchair controls[20]
- Provides a weightbearing surface for the upper limbs to assist in upper body support
- Protects arm from possible trauma in patients with sensory neglect[21]
- Increases awareness of an arm in patients with sensory neglect[21]

Disadvantages

- Lap boards may interfere with the patient's ability to propel the wheelchair, reach for wheel locks, and transfer out of the wheelchair. Consider having the sides of the board narrowed near the wheels to improve reach for the wheels.

- Board adds weight to the wheelchair. (This is no small matter. I have been accosted in the street by a mother who complained about the weight of her daughter's lap board.)
- Board may interfere with visual and tactile exploration of body parts.
- A lap board may act as a restraint if patient cannot independently remove it.

Comments

- Lap boards are either solid (nonclear) or clear. Consider a clear board for patients with adequate vision so they can see their lower limbs through the board surface.
- If the patient performs upper-limb skills, make sure the armrests are adjustable in height so that the lap board can be optimally positioned for UE activities.
- If there is a history of injury due to the limbs or head hitting the tray surface, consider padding the surface causing injury (i.e., pad top of board for head and upper-limb injury and pad under the board for knee banging). The lap board can also cause pressure to the trunk if patient slides forward into it. Address the problem of sliding by stabilizing the pelvis. If the problem persists, consider padding the inner rim of the lap board to protect the trunk.
- If the board is too low, the board may not provide enough support for the upper limb or sufficient clearance for knees. In addition, it may force the patient to strain to view objects at the lower visual level.

- If the board is too high, it may force the patient's shoulders up toward the ears (scapula elevation). Consider a board height from the seat equal to the distance from the top of the seat cushion to the elbow (with the arm vertically aligned) plus 1 in.[22]
- If there is too much of a gap between the abdomen and the inside of the board, the patient's arm may get caught between the board and the trunk. In addition, food or other objects may fall through this space if the gap is too wide. Although needs may vary, consider about a 1-in. gap between the abdomen and the inside of the board.
- If there is not enough gap between the abdomen and the inside of the board, the patient may not have enough space for winter coats, weight changes, and breathing.

PROTRACTION BLOCKS

Protraction blocks (shoulder protraction wings,[4] humeral blocks[3]) are rigid pads mounted posterior-laterally on the lap board or the back of the frame (Figure 7.10).

Indications

- Encourage midline posture on the UEs[4]
- May prevent the shoulders from extending behind the wheelchair
- May prevent excessive scapula retraction by blocking associated horizontal abduction at the shoulder

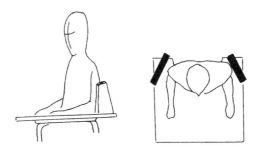

Fig. 7.10 Protraction blocks can encourage midline positioning of the upper extremities.

Comments

- Protraction blocks are useful on backward tilt-in-space wheelchairs because gravity tends to pull the patient's UEs into extension as the frame tilts backwards.
- Some patients are able to lift their UEs over the protraction blocks.
- The clinician may have to "play around" with the placement of the protraction blocks before the best location for a particular patient is determined.

HIP GUIDES

Hip guides (hip blocks) are support structures located on the sides of the seat near the hips (Figure 7.11).

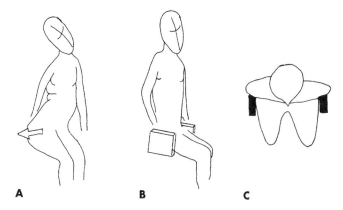

A   **B**   **C**

Fig. 7.11   Hip guides help center the patient's pelvis toward the center of the seat to encourage midline posture while sitting. A. Patient with the pelvis deviated out of midline without hip guides. B. Patient using hip guides with pelvis centered and trunk in midline. C. Patient with hip guides (aerial view).

Indications

- Guide the hips and pelvis toward the center of the seat
- Encourage midline positioning of the upper body

Disadvantages

- Increase weight of the wheelchair
- Decrease the functional width of the seat because the guides take up space

Comments

- If hip guides are positioned *too close together* (i.e., less than the hip-to-hip width of the patient), pressure sores can develop at the hip (greater trochanters). Transfers into a wheelchair may also be more difficult.
- If hip guides are positioned *too far apart* (i.e., greater than about 1 in. from each hip), they may not function to guide the pelvis toward the center of the seat, causing the patient to sit asymmetrically.

KNEE ADDUCTORS

Knee adductors (lateral thigh supports[1]) are support structures located on the sides of the seat near each knee (Figure 7.12).

Indication

- Prevents hips from abducting excessively

Disadvantage

- Adds weight to the wheelchair

Comments

- Make sure the knee adductor does not cause excessive pressure on the common peroneal nerve at the level of the fibula head.

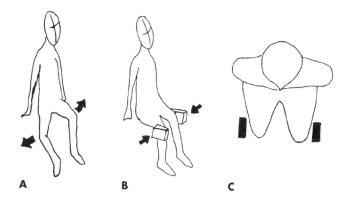

Fig. 7.12 A. Patient with excessive hip abduction (i.e., "frog" position of lower extremities). B. Knee adductors block excessive hip abduction of the lower extremities. C. Patient with knee adductors (aerial view).

- If the knee adductors are positioned *too close together* so that the knees are pressed together, it may be more difficult to transfer into the wheelchair. In addition, adductor contractures and poor hip-joint development may be promoted.
- If the knee adductors are positioned *too far apart* and do not touch the lateral knee, they may not be functioning to block undesirable hip abduction and hence may promote contractures of the hip abductors and external rotators.

ANTERIOR KNEE BLOCKS

Anterior knee blocks are padded structures in front of each knee that prevent anterior displacement of the knees and therefore indirectly prevent forward pelvic sliding.

Comments

- Interferes with transfers
- Deleterious effects if forces acting between the knee block and knee are excessive or if hip or femoral pathology exists
- Soft tissue inflammation possible from repetitive rubbing of knees against knee blocks

POMMELS

A pommel (medial leg separator, medial thigh separator,[1] medial knee block[3]) is a padded structure located between the knees (Figure 7.13).

Indications

- Prevents hip adductor contractures by keeping knees apart
- Prevents knees from pressing together, which can result in pressure sores
- Maintains hip joints in an abducted position for normal development and reduces the possibility of hip subluxation or dislocation[4]

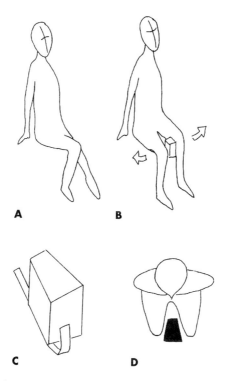

A   **B**

C   **D**

Fig. 7.13 The pommel helps promote normal hip development and minimize the possibility of adduction contractures. A. Patient without pommel exhibits a lower extremity scissoring pattern. B. Patient with pommel maintains hip abduction and knees apart. C. Pommel with hardware. D. Patient with pommel (aerial view).

Disadvantages

- A pommel interferes with transfers. Consider a removable pommel.
- Groin pressure and discomfort may occur if patient slides forward into the pommel.
- A pommel adds weight to the wheelchair.
- A patient who kicks or presses his or her knees together and into pommel hardware (metal) can sustain injuries (bruising). (In these cases, try to "hide" hardware under seat or pad hardware.)

Comments

- *Keep the pommel placement distal.* The pommel should not be located near the patient's groin area. Proximal placement may stimulate the hip adductors.[4]
- If the pommel is positioned *too far posteriorly* in the seat, groin pressure can result.
- If the pommel is positioned *too far anteriorly* in the seat, it may be located in front of the patient's knees and therefore not function to keep the knees apart.
- If the pommel is *too wide*, the patient who is flexible may be forced into excessive hip abduction.
- If the patient has tight knee adductors, then a wide pommel can cause pressure sores over the medial condyles of the knees.
- The pommel should not be used to prevent sliding out of wheelchairs because groin injuries can result.

WHEEL LOCKS

Wheel locks[23] (brakes, parking locks[2]) are metal devices on each side of the wheelchair that press into the rear tires.

Indications

- Locks the rear wheels to prevent the wheelchair from moving
- Provides stability during transfers[5]

Types

Toggle and level[2] are two different wheel-lock designs found on wheelchairs.

Toggle

Toggle design requires the user to apply anterior or posterior forces to engage the wheel lock. The amount of compression of the lock against the tire is preset (Figure 7.14A).[3]

Toggle-type wheel locks come in two varieties, depending on which direction the patient wishes to lock them. If the patient can self-propel the wheelchair, consider pull-to-lock wheel locks, so that the wheel locks are not accidentally locked as the patient pushes the wheels forward.

Level

Level wheel-lock designs require coordination[3] and some medial and lateral manipulation by the user to engage the

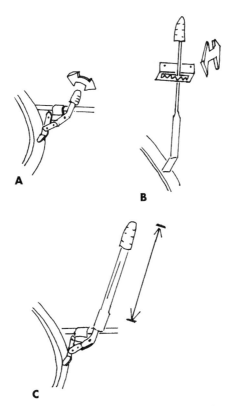

Fig. 7.14 A. Toggle wheel locks have a preset tension and require a pulling or pushing force. B. Level wheel locks have variable set tension against the tires and require some medial and lateral manipulation to operate. C. A brake extension facilitates reach and gives the patient a mechanical advantage to engage the wheel lock.

lock into notches (Figure 7.14B). The amount of compression of the lock against the tire (and therefore the "holding power") is variable and depends on which notch is selected.[3]

Location on Frame[12]

- *High mount*: easier to reach but may interfere with propulsion
- *Low mount*: requires better hand function and is harder to reach, but does not interfere with propulsion; there is a reduced risk of injuries to fingers during rapid propulsion[13]

Attendant-Operated Wheel Locks

Attendant-operated wheel locks allow easy access to the wheel locks for the attendant (i.e., attached toward the rear of the wheelchair) but not easy access for the patient.

Grade-Aid Mechanism

Grade-aid mechanisms may be ordered to facilitate forward propulsion up hill, to maintain forward momentum, and to prevent backward rolling.[9]

Brake Extensions

Brake extensions[18] are 6- to 9-in. extended, removable, metal arms that attach to the wheel locks. Brake extensions facilitate reach and provide a mechanical advantage to engage wheel locks (Figure 7.14C).

- The long lever length of the brake extension can cause excessive torque that can result in damage to the brake. Teach patients not to use excessive manual force.
- Because brake extensions are located near the rear wheels and extend into the air, they may interfere with manual propulsion and transfer activities.[3]
- Brake extensions can potentially be used as weapons by aggressive patients because they are removable. Consider having brake extensions attached to the frame by a chain.

Comments

- *Wheel locks must be locked for safety whenever the patient transfers in or out of the wheelchair.* (Patients have sustained serious injuries [hip fractures] because their unlocked wheelchair rolled away during a transfer.)
- The wheelchair can still move (slide) if the wheel locks are engaged but the floor is waxed or slippery. In these cases, have someone stand behind the wheelchair to keep it from sliding during patient transfers.
- During bus transportation, wheel locks alone are not enough. The bus driver must also secure the frame of the wheelchair to the floor of the bus for safety. Otherwise, the entire wheelchair can move if the bus stops abruptly.

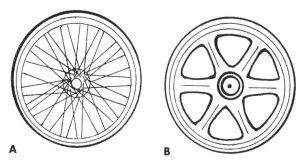

Fig. 7.15   A. Spoke wheels are lightweight but require maintenance.
B. Molded (spokeless) wheels require low maintenance and are durable,
but are heavier than spoke wheels.

REAR WHEELS

Rear wheels[18] enable the wheelchair to roll.

Types

Spoke

See Figure 7.15A.

- Lighter weight[9]
- Require maintenance

Molded (Spokeless)

See Figure 7.15B.

- Slightly heavier[3]

- Low maintenance[2]
- More durable[9]

Size

Rear wheel size ranges from 20 in. to 26 in. in diameter. As diameter increases, turning radius increases and maneuvering becomes more difficult.
- Standard size: 24-in. diameter
- Hemiplegic chairs: 22-in. diameter

Wheel Angle

Wheel angle (camber[18]) refers to the angle of the rear wheels. The top of the wheel is tilted medially while the bottom of wheel is tilted laterally. Angling the rear wheels can improve the patient's push efficiency[13] and the lateral stability of the wheelchair,[9,13] but increase the width of the wheelchair, which can potentially limit access through doorways.

Advantages

- Improves push efficiency[13]
- Increases stability of wheelchair when turning[13] and during long reaches[9]
- Easier to steer[13]
- Improves reach of handrims

Disadvantage

- Increases width of wheelchair; may make going through doors difficult[13]

REAR TIRES

Rear tires[13, 18] provide a rolling surface, traction, and shock absorption for rear wheels. The three major categories are *pneumatic* (air filled), *solid rubber tires*, and *airless* (solid insert).

Types

Pneumatic[24]

- Good shock absorption
- Comfortable ride[2]
- Prolongs life of wheelchair[2]
- Lighter in weight
- Use on carpet, gravel, and grass
- Outdoor use[9]
- Use on uneven ground[9]
- Maintenance problems (e.g., punctures[3]) (Consider purchasing an air pump.[3])

Solid Rubber Tires

- Indoor use[2]
- Durable[3]
- No maintenance problems
- Less shock absorption
- Use on smooth surfaces[2]
- Use on hard floors (e.g., nursing home)[9]

Airless (Solid Insert)[18]

- No maintenance problems

- Shock absorption; better than solid rubber but not as good as pneumatics

Tire Tread

- Improves traction[9]
- Use on soft, sandy, and rough terrain[2]

HANDRIMS

Handrims are circular tubes attached to rear wheels.[2]

Indications

- Provides a grip surface for self-propulsion
- Controls soiling of hands

Size

The size of the handrims acts in a similar way to the gears on a bicycle and provides either a speed or power advantage.[9]

Small-Diameter Rims

- Speed advantage[9] (good for sports)
- Easier to maintain speed[13]

Large-Diameter Rims

- Power advantage[9] (good if the patient is weak)
- Starts and acceleration are easier[13]

Types of Handrims

- *Standard* (uncoated)
- *Vinyl or plastic coated*:
  Provide firm, comfortable grip on handrims for self-propulsion[3, 13]
  Can cause finger burns due to the increased friction coefficient of handrim coating[13]
- *Projections*:
  Assist propulsion if difficulty gripping or hand deformity
  Vary in spacing,[9] orientation (i.e., vertical or oblique),[9] and shape (knobs)[3]

SPOKEGUARD[18]

A spokeguard is a covering over the outer spokes of each wheel to protect the fingers. If spokeguards do not offer sufficient protection from finger injury, consider ordering spokeless wheels.

CASTERS

Casters[18] are small wheels, usually in the front, that enable wheelchairs to turn and steer (Figure 7.16).

Size

Caster size ranges from 2 in. to 8 in. in diameter.

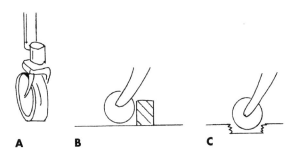

Fig. 7.16 A. Casters enable the wheelchair to turn and steer. B, C. Small casters do not roll over obstacles well and can become caught in cracks.

Larger Casters

- Better shock absorption (better ride)
- Less maneuverability
- Rolls easier over obstacles[13]
- Lowers rolling resistance[25]

Smaller Casters

- Smaller turning radius for easier and quicker turning (good for sports)[9, 13]
- Minimal flutter[13]
- Clears front rigging (foot plates) better than larger casters
- More easily caught in potholes and sidewalk cracks[3]
- Less shock absorption (rougher ride)[13]

Wider (Ball-Shaped) Casters

- Improve rolling resistance and use on sand[25]

Pin Locks

Pin locks help to stabilize the casters during transfers.[3]

CASTER TIRES

Caster tires[18] provide a rolling surface, traction, and shock absorption for casters.

Types

Pneumatic

- Good shock absorption
- Comfortable ride[3]
- Lightweight[3]
- Maintenance problems (i.e., punctures[3])
- Use outdoors[2, 13, 24]

Solid Tires

- No maintenance problems
- Less shock absorption
- Use indoors[2]

Semipneumatics

- Comfortable ride
- Puncture proof but heavier and more difficult to propel[3]

- Use outdoors[2]

SEAT BELTS

A seat belt (positioning belt[3] or pelvic belt[1]) is a strap on the seat that is secured across the patient's hips.

Indications

- Safety during transportation
- Used as a positioning belt[3] to maintain proper body alignment and pelvic position
- Prevents forward sliding in the wheelchair
- Lower extremity (LE) extensor thrust[13]

Types

Choose a buckle (fastener) that can be easily operated by the patient.

- *Hook and loop fasteners*: require grasp and pulling to open belt (Although I have seen this fastener used on a seat belt, it probably is not strong or safe enough.)
- *Buckle with movable tongue*: requires grasp and pull to open belt (Figure 7.17A)
- *Airplane* (lift the handle to open): may require wrist extension or shoulder external rotation to open belt (Figure 7.17B)
- *Molded clip* (opens when the sides are squeezed): requires opposition of thumb and digits to open belt (Figure 7.17C)

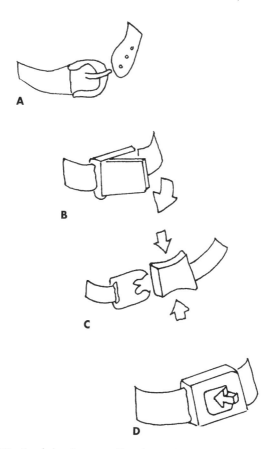

Fig. 7.17 Seat belt styles. A. Buckle with movable tongue. B. Airplane. C. Molded clip. D. Auto belt.

- *Auto* (push the button to open): may require finger extension, wrist flexion, or shoulder internal rotation to open belt (Figure 7.17D)

Size

- Small children: 1-in. wide[3]
- Large children: 1.5-in. wide[3]
- Adults: 2-in. wide[3]
- Large or obese adults: extra long

Orientation of Seat Belts and Other Pelvic Positioning Devices

- *Peroneal straps*: additional straps (wrapped around each thigh, usually in a medial to lateral direction); may help discourage forward sliding of the pelvis (Figure 7.18A). Avoid compression of sensitive structures such as the femoral artery.[3]
- *45 degrees*: usually effective in maintaining pelvic positioning (Figure 7.18C).
- *90 degrees*: less restrictive, enables pelvis to anteriorly tilt.[3]
- *Attendant-operated belt*: provides convenient belt access for the caregiver when the patient cannot operate the seat belt (Figure 7.18D).

Disadvantage

- Seat belts may act as a restraint if the patient cannot independently operate the belt. Try to order a buckle

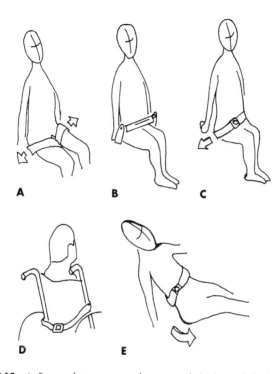

Fig. 7.18 A. Peroneal straps, secured across each thigh, can help discourage forward sliding of the pelvis. B. The sub anterior superior iliac spine bar is an aggressive approach to maintaining pelvic positioning in a patient who exhibits very strong extensor activity and forward sliding behavior. C. Many patients generally do well with only a seat belt oriented at a 45-degree angle. D. Attendant-operated belt location offers easy access for the caregiver when the patient cannot operate the seat belt. E. If the seat belt is positioned across the waist instead of hips, forward sliding may occur.

that the patient can open and close independently. Also, have the buckle installed in a location the patient can reach. Buckles positioned near the greater trochanters may be too difficult for the patient to operate.

Comments

- The seat belt is typically attached to the frame of the wheelchair with the belt angles 45 degrees up from the seat to maintain a midline pelvis.[4] Another option is to secure the seat belt at a 90-degree angle to the seat.
- If the seat belt is too high (i.e., at the level of the umbilicus), the patient may be able to "do the limbo" and slide underneath the seat belt (Figure 7.18E). Make sure the seat belt is positioned across the hips and not the waist. If the buckle is at the level of the umbilicus, it is too high!
- If the patient has a bony pelvis, consider placing a pressure-reducing pad between the buckle and the patient.
- If the seat belt is too loose, the patient could slide forward until he or she makes contact with the belt. *This is probably the most common reason why patients slide.* As a rough guide, tighten seat belts so that you can only fit two fingers of thickness between the belt and the patient's abdomen.

SUB ANTERIOR SUPERIOR ILIAC SPINE BAR

The sub anterior superior iliac spine bar (pelvic stabilizer) is a rigid pelvic restraint (i.e., a round, padded, metal bar) positioned below the patient's anterior superior iliac spine (ASIS) (Figure 7.18B).[15]

Indication

- To prevent strong extensor thrusting out of the wheelchair

Disadvantages

- May be difficult for caregiver to install and remove bar
- Interferes with independent transfers

Comments

- Some patients with severe extensor activity may actually bend the metal bar.
- It may be difficult to properly position the bar below the ASIS.
- Monitor the patient's skin for pressure sores on the anterior pelvis.

FRONT RIGGING

Front rigging (foot support[1]) is a term that refers to both the footrest and legrest.[2] Front rigging provides a support surface for the feet and consists of a support bracket and foot plate (Figure 7.19).[23]

Indications

- Prevents feet from dragging on floor during transportation[2]
- Supports the distal thigh from pressure at the front edge of the seat so that restricted circulation in that region is prevented[2]

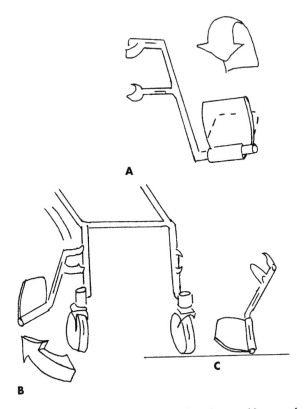

Fig. 7.19 Front rigging features. A. Flip-up foot plates enable access for transfers. B. Swing-away front rigging enables better access for transfers but is less durable and adds weight. C. Detachable front rigging improves maneuverability in small spaces.

- Places the knee joint in the required angle of knee extension or flexion
- Supports the ankle joint in the required amount of dorsiflexion

Types[12, 13]

- *Fixed front rigging with flip-up foot plates*: durable; enables access for transfers but does not swing away for use in tight quarters.[18] A flip-up feature (Figure 7.19A) enables access for transfers.
- *Swing-away*: better access for transfers but less durable and increased weight (Figure 7.19B).
- *Detachable*: for maneuvering into small spaces[2] (i.e., bathrooms) (Figure 7.19C).
- *Elevating legrest*: supports both leg and foot at multiple knee-angle positions and may be indicated for casted legs, arthrodesed knees, edema,[2] and for orthostatic hypotension.[18] Elevating legrests, however, increase both weight and overall length of the wheelchair and are contraindicated if the patient presents with hamstring tightness.[3]

Angle of Front Rigging

- *90-degree*: The support bracket is fixed and angled at 90 degrees from a horizontal plane to provide 90-degree knee flexion while sitting (Figure 7.20A). Hamstrings are placed on slack and knee flexion contractures are accommodated more in 90-degree than in 70-degree brackets.

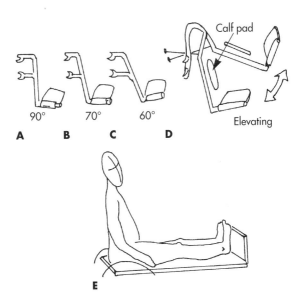

Fig. 7.20 Angle of front rigging. A. 90-degree front rigging helps place tight hamstrings on slack. B. Standard front rigging is fixed at 70 degrees. C. 60 degree front rigging provides better caster clearance but increases wheelchair length. D. Elevating legrests have adjustable angles to enable adjustable limb elevation. E. Custom lower-extremity panels elevate and fix the lower extremities in extension but make transfers difficult.

- *70-degree*: A standard support bracket is fixed and angled at 70 degrees from a horizontal plane (Figure 7.20B).
- *60-degree*: The support bracket is fixed and angled at 60 degrees from a horizontal plane, thus improving caster

clearance but increasing overall wheelchair length (Figure 7.20C).[18]

- *Elevating* (adjustable angle): The support bracket is adjustable and elevates or lowers the limb (Figure 7.20D). Length of support bracket needs to be adjusted following change in angle of elevation.
- *Elevated* (fixed angle): Nonadjustable custom panels support the LEs when knees are fixed in extension (Figure 7.20E). A nonadjustable, fixed-angle panel can interfere with transfers and increase overall length and weight of the wheelchair.

Foot Plates and Supports

Standard Foot Plates

With standard foot plates, each foot is supported in a neutral ankle position (Figure 7.21A).

One-Piece Foot Board

If a patient is strong and tends to break foot plates, consider installing a one-piece foot board across both foot plates to strengthen foot support, or request reinforcing the foot plates with hardware or welding (Figure 7.21B). (Note that welding renders the attachment permanent and nonadjustable.)

- Provides a more stable surface[3]
- Provides a larger foot-support area
- May increase support strength

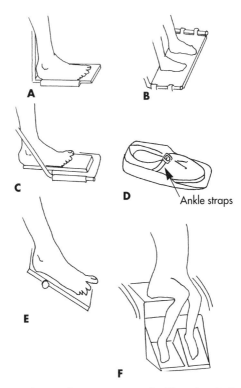

Fig. 7.21 Foot plates and supports. A. Standard foot plate. B. One-piece foot board offers greater stability and surface area. C. Foot plate extenders help accommodate hamstring tightness. D. Foot sandals provide a secure foot placement. E. Adjustable-angle foot plates accommodate limited foot and ankle range. F. Custom footbox accommodates bilateral lower extremity asymmetry.

- Can be swing-away for transfers
- May interfere with independent transfers
- Adds weight to frame

Foot Plate Extenders

If the foot plates are located too far forward relative to the feet or the patient has knee flexion contractures, consider extending the foot plates posteriorly and under the wheelchair, using foot plate extenders, so feet are adequately supported (Figure 7.21C).

Foot Sandals

If the patient's feet need to remain positioned but are difficult to stabilize with straps, consider foot sandals. Sandals provide greater contact and support by surrounding the border of each foot and securing the foot with straps (Figure 7.21D).

Adjustable-Angle Foot Plates

If the ankles are fixed in dorsiflexion or plantarflexion, consider angle-adjustable foot plates to accommodate the deformity (Figure 7.21E).

Custom Foot Box

If the patient has a fixed LE deformity resulting in foot locations that cannot be supported by conventional front rigging, consider a custom foot box that can provide individual support for each foot (Figure 7.21F).

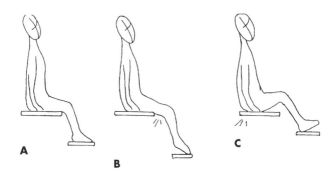

Fig. 7.22 A. Adequate foot plate height without excessive pressures under thigh or buttocks. B. If foot plate is adjusted too low, excessive pressure at distal posterior thigh and forward pelvic sliding can occur. C. If foot plate is adjusted too high, excessive ischial pressure, heel pressure, and pressure sores can occur.

Foot Plate Height

The foot plate should support the weight of the lower limb and allow the thighs to rest parallel to the seat surface without excessive pressure distally under the thigh or proximally under the buttocks (Figure 7.22A).

If the Foot Plate Is Too Low

If the foot plate is too low, the feet may hang, causing excessive pressure under the distal thighs, resulting in restricted circulation.[2] The patient may also slide forward in the seat (Figure 7.22B).

If the Foot Plate Is Too High

If the foot plate is too high, so that the distal thigh no longer contacts the seat, excessive ischial pressure and potential pressure-sore development at the ischia, coccyx, sacrum, or heels may result (Figure 7.22C).

Comments

- If the patient wears shoes with braces, make sure the foot plates are large enough.
- If the foot plates are low to the floor, they may interfere with the casters' capability of rotating. Family members may complain that the wheelchair does not turn. Consider smaller casters or 60-degree support brackets if the patient has sufficient hamstring length.
- If the patient has knee extension contractures and cannot flex the knees to 70 degrees from full extension, an elevating legrest may be needed to support the LE.
- Avoid pressure of the front rigging on the patient's common peroneal nerve at the level of the fibula head.
- Patients and caregivers tend to trip over front rigging if it cannot be removed during transfers. Consider swing-away or detachable features to avoid accidents.
- Elevating legrests are heavier than footrests, can make the wheelchair longer, and can shift the center of gravity of the wheelchair forward when elevated, thereby making it easier to tip the frame forward.

HEEL LOOPS

Heel loops (see Chapter 1; Figure 1.1) are nonrigid, semi-circularly shaped material located on the rear portion of each foot plate behind the patient's heels.

Indication

- To prevent the feet from falling behind the foot plates

Comments

- Consider stiffer heel loop material if heel loops lose their shape and flatten over time.
- If the patient's feet fall behind the foot plate with heel loops in use, consider a higher (i.e., taller) heel loop, calf strap, or calf panel, or construct a back wall for the foot plate.
- If the patient vigorously lifts and lowers the foot onto the foot plate (i.e., stomps feet), make sure hardware (i.e., bolts) that secures the heel loop to the foot plate does not cause injury to the foot.

ANKLE STRAPS

Ankle straps are small belts that secure the foot and ankle to the foot plates (see Figure 7.21D).

Indications

- Prevents foot from falling from foot plates
- Maintains flexed lower-limb alignment of the ankle and knee in the wheelchair

- Positions LEs in patients with significant spasticity[9]

Disadvantages

- Limits freedom of movement (i.e., kicking movements)
- Interferes with independent transfers

Comments

- An ankle strap angle at 45 degrees encourages pressure toward the heel and may help to inhibit a positive support reaction.[4]
- Strong patients may break through hook-and-loop–secured straps. Consider belt buckles with a movable tongue and a leather strap for strong patients but make sure the metal buckle either does not cause skin irritation or is sufficiently padded.
- Ankle straps function best and are probably tolerated better if the patient wears shoes or sneakers rather than socks or bare feet.
- Ankle straps should be long enough to fit around the patient wearing shoes with braces.
- Patients with LE flexor activity may slide forward in the wheelchair if ankle straps are used, because the patient may attempt to pull up his or her feet while anchored to the foot plates.

CALF PAD

A calf pad is a flat rigid support located on front rigging (i.e., elevating legrests) at the level of the calf (see Figure 7.20D).

Indication

- Physical support for the calf when the legrest is elevated[2]

Comment

- Calf pads are primarily used on elevating legrests.

CALF STRAP

A calf strap is a nonrigid support that is suspended across the support bracket of the front rigging and is situated behind the patient's calf (see Chapter 1; Figure 1.1).

Indications

- Discourage the feet from falling behind the foot plates and under the wheelchair
- May be useful in patients with LE flexor activity or in patients who do not tolerate heel loops and ankle straps

Disadvantage

- May interfere with the ability of front rigging to swing away

REAR ANTI-TIPPERS

Rear anti-tippers (anti-tipper extensions[13]) are metal tubes with small wheels that attach to the rear of the wheelchair near the floor (see Chapter 1; Figure 1.1).

Indication

- Use for safety to prevent the wheelchair from tipping backward[2]

Disadvantages

- Anti-tippers tend to become lost easily if not secured in place.
- Anti-tippers tend to break if people step on them (e.g., to raise front wheels up a curb).
- Caregivers pushing wheelchair may hit the front of their legs into anti-tippers. Warn the caregiver ahead of time.
- Anti-tippers may interfere with mobility (e.g., "popping a wheelie") in active wheelchair users.

Comments

- Wheelchair-related fatalities are associated with tipping of the wheelchair.[16]
- Anti-tippers are helpful, but they do not work if they are pointed toward the ceiling. Keep them pointed toward the floor except when going up curbs.
- If the patient tends to tip the wheelchair forward, consider *front anti-tippers*, which attach to the front of the frame. Front anti-tippers, however, may interfere during ramp and curb negotiation.
- If the patient tends to tip the wheelchair sideways, you have a problem. Sideways anti-tippers are not common. Consider widening the wheelchair's base of support by

adjusting the camber of the rear wheels, adding a thicker wheel, or obtaining a wider frame if absolutely necessary. Even then, the patient should be monitored. I have seen a few patients with Huntington's chorea tip wheelchairs regardless of efforts to prevent it.

SHORT TIPPING LEVER

The short tipping lever[13] is tubing on the rear of the frame, near the floor, which the caretaker steps down on with one foot to raise the front wheels (i.e., casters) in the air to negotiate curbs.

PUSH HANDLES

Push handles[9] may be optional but are required for attendant-operated wheelchairs. Independent, active wheelchair users may find push handles degrading (see Figure 1.1).

STORAGE

Utility Bag

- If the patient needs to carry medically related supplies (i.e., diapers, medication), consider ordering a bag to hang from the rear of the wheelchair.

Storage Rack

- If the patient uses an assistive device (i.e., cane, crutches) or oxygen equipment, consider ordering a storage rack to be installed on the wheelchair.

Feeding Pole

- If the patient is continuously fed through a tube, consider ordering a feeding pole attachment.

EXERCISES

1. The hospital where you consult is instituting a policy whereby all patients at risk for pressure sores will receive a gel cushion on admission. Do you agree with this policy? Why or why not?

2. A study reports a "significant" reduction in the ischial pressure of spinal cord patients when using an air cushion as compared with a gel or foam cushion. On reading the study more carefully, you discover that the researchers did not report the reliability of their pressure-measuring sensor and that six subjects participated in the study (three persons with quadriplegia and three with paraplegia). What do you conclude from this study? Are you going to recommend air cushions for your spinal cord patients based on this finding?

3. It is late on a Friday afternoon, and you are evaluating a patient for a new anterior trunk support (i.e., vest harness) and a neck ring. Do you dispense the equipment to the patient and ask staff on Monday how the patient did, or do you wait and reevaluate this patient on a future date?

4. A patient is referred to you for chronic sliding in the wheelchair. What might you first measure on the wheelchair? (Hint: a seat dimension.)

REFERENCES

1. Trefler E, Hobson DA, Taylor SJ, et al. Seating and Mobility for Persons with Physical Disabilities. Tucson, AZ: Therapy Skill Builders, 1993;242–248.

2. Wilson AB, McFarland SR. Types of wheelchairs. J Rehabil Res Dev 1990;2(suppl):104–116.

3. Bergen AF, Presperin J, Tallman T. Positioning for Function: Wheelchairs and Other Assistive Technologies. Valhalla, NY: Valhalla Rehabilitation Publications, 1990;13–82.

4. Taylor SJ. Evaluating the client with physical disabilities for wheelchair sitting. Am J Occup Ther 1987;41:711–716.

5. Harrymann SE, Warren LR. Positioning and Power Mobility. In G Church, S Glennen (eds), The Handbook of Assistive Technologies. San Diego: Singular, 1992;55–92.

6. Jarvis S. Wheelchair clinics for children. Physiotherapy 1985;71:132–134.

7. Brubaker C. Ergonometric considerations. J Rehabil Res Dev 1990;2(suppl):37–48.

8. Grunewald J. Wheelchair selection from a nursing perspective. Rehabil Nurs 1986;11:31–32.

9. Currie DM, Hardwick K, Marburger RA, Britell CW. Wheelchair Prescription and Adaptive Seating. In JL Delisa, BM Gans (eds), Rehabilitation Medicine: Principles and Practice (2nd ed). Philadelphia: Lippincott, 1993;563–585.

10. Garber SL. Classification of wheelchair cushions. Am J Occup Ther 1979;10:652–654.

11. Garber SL. Wheelchair cushions: a historical review. Am J Occup Ther 1985;39:453–459.

12. Kohlmeyer KM, Yarkony GM. Functional Outcomes After Spinal Cord Injury Rehabilitation. In GM Yarkony (ed), Spinal Cord Injury: Medical Management and Rehabilitation. Gaithersburg, MD: Aspen, 1994;9–14.

13. Ragnarsson KT. Clinical perspectives on wheelchair selection: prescription considerations and a comparison of conventional and light weight wheelchairs. J Rehabil Res Dev 1990;2(suppl):8–16.

14. Panel for the Prediction and Prevention of Pressure Ulcers in Adults. Pressure Ulcers in Adults: Prediction and Prevention. Clinical Practice Guideline, no. 3. AHCPR pub. no. 92-0047. Rockville,

MD: Agency for Heath Care Policy and Research, Public Health Service, U.S. Department of Health and Human Services, 1992;13–30.

15. Redford JB. Seating and wheeled mobility in the disabled elderly population. Arch Phys Med Rehabil 1993;74:877–885.

16. Calder CJ, Kirby RL. Fatal wheelchair-related accidents in the United States. Am J Phys Med Rehabil 1990;69:184–190.

17. Rubin BS, Dube AH, Mitchell EK. Asphyxial deaths due to physical restraint: a case series. Arch Fam Med 1993;2:405–408.

18. Kohlmeyer KM, Stevens S, Ueberfluss J. Wheelchairs. In GM Yarkony (ed), Spinal Cord Injury: Medical Management and Rehabilitation. Gaithersburg, MD: Aspen, 1994;169–172.

19. Brant J. Wheelchair clinics work. Occup Ther Health Care 1988;5:67–70.

20. Warren CG. Technical considerations: power mobility and its implications. J Rehabil Res Dev 1990;2(suppl):74–85.

21. Mattingly D. Wheelchair selection. Orthop Nurs 1993;12:11–17.

22. Kamenetz HL. The Wheelchair Book: Mobility for the Disabled. Springfield, IL: Thomas, 1969;132–134.

23. Wheelchair Prescription: Care and Service (booklet no. 4). Los Angeles: Everest & Jennings, Inc., 1976;8.

24. Behrman AL. Clinical perspectives on wheelchair selection: factors in functional assessment. J Rehabil Res Dev 1990;2(suppl):17–27.

25. Hillman M. Wheelchair wheels for use on sand. Med Engineer Physics 1994;16:243–247.

IV

Common Wheelchair Problems

Evidence of a Problem

You can tell a lot about a wheelchair's past by looking at its scars. This is where you can play detective.

WORN PARTS

The location of wear on the seat cushion indicates how the patient typically sits. If the patient sits properly, then the seat eventually wears symmetrically toward the rear of the seat. If the front of the seat is worn, it suggests that the patient slides forward and may sit on his or her back-side (sacrum). If the seat is worn on one side, it suggests that the patient is sitting with excessive pressure over one hip (Figure 8.1).

- *Seat worn in front*: patient sliding forward
- *Seat worn on one side*: patient sitting asymmetrically
- *Seat worn in center rear*: patient sitting in the center

BROKEN PARTS

Chronically broken parts indicate *a weak link* in the wheelchair. Either the patient (or caregiver) is too rough on the part or the wheelchair part is a lemon (defective

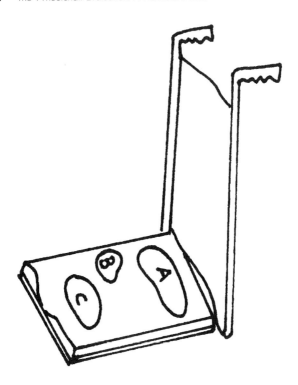

Fig. 8.1 A worn seat can suggest where the patient habitually sits on the cushion. A. Wear in center rear of cushion suggests a proper sitting position. B. Wear on one side suggests asymmetric sitting over one hip. C. Wear in front suggests sliding activity and possible sacral sitting.

design). Consider reinforcing the part or changing the design and educating everyone on its proper use.

COMMON PROBLEMS AND POSSIBLE CAUSES

This section reviews common wheelchair problems that you are likely to encounter. There are often many causes of a wheelchair problem and therefore many solutions. Note that many problems can be solved by simply positioning the patient properly in the wheelchair. It is therefore always a good idea to first properly position the patient before solving a wheelchair problem.

Sliding Out of Wheelchair

Sliding generally occurs when a force (muscular or gravitational) pushes the body forward in the wheelchair. Sliding is a problem because sacral sitting may result, pressure sores can develop, and the patient will be less able to perform skills well when poorly supported. There is also the danger that the patient may be injured from sliding. A typical example is the patient whose neck becomes entangled in a chest harness while sliding. Deaths have been reported as a result of strangulation from physical restraints.[1]

Possible Causes

- Patient was not properly positioned in the wheelchair.
- There is no seat belt.
- Seat belt is loose, broken, or not being used.
- Seat is too deep (long) for the patient.

- Seat is too shallow (short) for the patient.
- Patient's hip flexion range of motion is limited.
- Patient has hamstring tightness.
- Patient has been sitting too long.
- Patient wishes to get out of the wheelchair.
- Patient is in pain or discomfort from the wheelchair.
- Patient performs extreme flexion or extension movements of the lower extremities.
- Extensor tone is marked.
- Foot plates are too low and do not support feet.
- Curved seat cushion is backwards (installed incorrectly).
- Seat is in a downward tilted angle (pitched forward).
- Clothing is slippery (low friction coefficient).

Head Falls Forward in the Wheelchair

A forward flexed head position is a problem because the patient's environment is not in view, feeding and school activities can be more difficult, and there is a danger that his or her chin may cover the air opening of a tracheotomy (if one exists). This problem is often due to poor head control. Try to address the problem when possible with gravity-assisted support (tilting backwards, reclining) rather than head and neck restraints.

<u>Possible Causes</u>

- Head control is poor.
- Patient is tired (fatigued).

- Patient wants to keep head forward.
- Neck range of motion is limited in extension.
- Patient is having a seizure.
- Patient is falling asleep.
- Patient is drowsy from effects of medication.
- Headrest is an irritant.
- Neck pain is present.
- Headrest is posted too far forward.

Trunk Leans (Listing) to the Side

Trunk listing can be intentional or beyond the patient's control.

Possible Causes

- Trunk control is poor.
- Patient wants to get out of the wheelchair.
- Patient is tired (fatigued).
- Patient is interested in something on the floor.
- Lateral trunk support is broken, poorly positioned, or absent.
- Patient is uncomfortable sitting.
- Patient is having a seizure.
- Patient is falling asleep.
- Scoliosis or limited trunk mobility is present.
- Patient has low muscle tone.
- Strength of trunk muscles is inadequate.
- Pathologic reflexes are active.

Wheelchair Tips Over (Backward)

Tipping is an obvious safety hazard (not to mention that it is scary).[2] Tipping problems are usually due to (1) a small base of support (frame), (2) a high center of mass (patient), or (3) a large force that pushes the center of mass beyond the base of support. Try to increase the base (frame) or lower the mass (seating system and patient) when possible.

Possible Causes

- Anti-tippers are not in use, are not pointed downward, are broken, or are not on the wheelchair.
- Patient rocks trunk or bangs head against the back of wheelchair.
- The seating system is installed too far back on the frame.
- Rear wheels are installed too far forward on the frame.
- The frame is too small for the patient.
- The patient is too large for the frame.
- Wheels are not level, worn unequally, or missing.
- Seating system is installed too high on frame.
- Heavy bags are being hung from the back of the wheelchair.
- Frame is bent.

Patient Is "Uncomfortable" in Wheelchair

One of the primary goals of any chair is comfort. Check to make sure the patient has adequate flexibility and padding to sit comfortably. Also check that wheelchair components are not causing excessive pressure.

Possible Causes

- Patient is not properly positioned in the wheelchair.
- Seat cushion is worn (bottomed out).
- Custom-molded cushions fit poorly.
- Wheelchair components are irritating or causing pressure.
- Discomfort is orthopedic related. Inspect for fracture or hip dislocation.
- Patient is sitting too long.
- Joint range of motion is inadequate to sit in wheelchair. Adjust seat and back position to accommodate tightness.
- Patient is bony. Consider a better pressure-reducing cushion.
- Orthotics (braces or body jackets) are irritating the patient in wheelchair.
- Patient is generally irritable from a change in medical status.

Patient "Hooks" Head Around Headrest

"Hooking" is a potentially dangerous activity. Patients may tend to lean to the side of the wheelchair and hook or move their head around to the outside of the headrest. At that point, the patient often becomes stuck in that position. Stabilizing the patient's pelvis and trunk often helps to address a head-hooking problem.

Possible Causes

- Patient was not properly positioned.
- Patient wants to look around the headrest.
- Patient has poor head control.
- Patient has poor trunk balance.
- Anterior trunk support is not adequate, enabling the patient's trunk to flex forward and then to the side.
- Lateral trunk supports are broken, poorly positioned, or absent, enabling the patient to lean sideways.
- Headrest is the wrong shape or not deep (long) enough.
- Neck (cervical) range of motion is excessive.
- Primitive reflexes are activated.
- Patient has scoliosis, resulting in trunk listing to side.
- Patient uses headrest as a form of stimulation.
- Headrest is an irritant, and the patient attempts to move away from it.
- Patient attempts to stabilize himself or herself by using his or her head. Try to better stabilize the pelvis and trunk.

Injuring Self in the Wheelchair

People love to blame the wheelchair when the patient is injured. Determine if the patient's injury was actually caused by the wheelchair.

Possible Causes

- Patient was not properly positioned in the wheelchair.
- Patient displays self-abusive behavior.

- There is excessive pressure from wheelchair parts.
- Hard, sharp, or moving wheelchair parts caused injury.
- Patient fell out of wheelchair (see Trunk Leans [Listing] to the Side and Wheelchair Tips Over [Backward])
- Patient injured self out of the wheelchair (i.e., not in the wheelchair).
- Injury caused by rough handling of the patient.
- Injury caused by normal handling of a patient with osteoporosis.
- Injury caused by physical abuse.

"Slumped" Sitting in Wheelchair

The patient's trunk may appear collapsed into flexion, his or her normal lumbar curve flattened, and he or she may be sitting on his or her sacrum rather than over the ischia.

Possible Causes

- Patient is not properly positioned in the wheelchair.
- Seat is too deep (very common).
- Patient prefers a slumped position.
- Patient sits too long (fatigued).
- Patient has fixed posterior (backward) pelvic tilt.
- Patient's muscle tone is low (i.e., has the feel of a rag doll).
- Back insert is spoon shaped, which allows the pelvis to tilt backwards.
- Back insert lacks lumbar support.

Wheelchair Is Too Small

A wheelchair that is too small is usually seen with children as they are still growing. After death and taxes, growth in children is almost a given. Try to build a couple of years' growth in a seating system if growth is anticipated.

Possible Causes

- Patient is not properly positioned in the wheelchair (i.e., pelvis is not positioned to the rear of the seat).
- Patient grew.
- Patient wears a new brace or body jacket that takes up space in the wheelchair.
- Patient is wearing thicker apparel (e.g., winter coats).
- The seat cushion shifted backward.
- The back insert shifted forward.

Wheelchair Does Not Fold

Possible Causes

- Family was never shown how to fold wheelchair (very common).
- Seat and back inserts were installed with nonremovable hardware (i.e., the seating system must be removed before the frame will fold).
- Wheelchair parts attached to the frame interfere with folding ability.
- Frame is bent.
- Frame is not designed to fold.

Wheel Locks (Brakes) Do Not Work

Wheel locks need to be repaired immediately (for safety) if they do not work, because injuries can occur if they are not engaged during transfers and bus transportation.

Possible Causes

- Wheel locks (hardware) loosened and do not contact the rubber tire.
- Wheel locks are broken (e.g., metal bent, hardware missing).
- Rubber or tread on rear tires is worn.
- Air pressure in pneumatic tires is low.
- Wheel locks are working but floor is slippery (i.e., waxed floors).

Wheelchair Is Difficult to Push

Possible Causes

- Wheel locks are locked or partially engaged.
- Pneumatic tires are flat.
- Wheels are rubbing against side of wheelchair (i.e., against the skirt guard).
- Casters are hitting the foot plate.
- Frame is bent (twisted).
- Bearings in wheels are worn (may also be noisy).
- Wheel axles are not aligned.
- Wheelchair is heavy.
- Patient's feet are dragging.

- Push handles are too low or too high for the caregiver.
- Patient's physical disability interferes with efficient self-propulsion.
- Rear wheels are not optimally positioned (i.e., too posterior) for efficient propulsion.
- There is friction from floor surface (i.e., carpet, gravel, snow, sand).
- There is increased rolling resistance of the wheels[3] secondary to small wheel diameter, thicker tires, low tire pressure, increased tire weight, or tire treads.
- Difficulty caused by wind.
- Difficulty caused by inclines.

REFERENCES

1. Rubin BS, Dube AH, Mitchell EK. Asphyxial deaths due to physical restraint: a case series. Arch Fam Med 1993;2:405–408.
2. Calder CJ, Kirby RL. Fatal wheelchair-related accidents in the United States. Am J Phys Med Rehabil 1990;69:184–190.
3. Kyle C. Mechanical Factors Affecting the Speed of a Cycle. In ER Burke (ed), Science of Cycling. Champaign, IL: Human Kinetics Books, 1986;123–136.

Appendixes

A1

Ethics: A Guiding Principle

Patients and their families may request that a new wheelchair be ordered. Because a wheelchair is an expensive piece of durable medical equipment, it may be helpful to have ethical guidance in considering a new wheelchair.

When is it fair to order a new wheelchair? Ethics is a branch of philosophy that deals with fairness and can help answer this question. Ethics was invented to help guide people in making fair or just decisions in a "civilized" world. Modern ethics recognizes two opposing schools of thought: the rights of the individual versus the greatest good of everyone (society).[1]

RIGHTS OF THE INDIVIDUAL

Clinicians and families need to consider the right of the patient to reach his or her fullest functional potential and to minimize the likelihood of illness (morbidity) and death (mortality). The guiding question for everyone can be

- Will the wheelchair or wheelchair component meaningfully improve the patient's function, reduce morbidity, or reduce mortality risk?

If the answer is yes, then the wheelchair can be justified and the rights of the individual can be advocated. One example would be a power wheelchair that allows safe and independent community mobility for an individual who would otherwise rely on others for help (function). A second example would be a gel seat cushion for an individual who lacks sensation and would otherwise be at risk for skin breakdown (morbidity). A third example is the wheelchair for a bedridden individual who could aspirate (i.e., choke) and die (e.g., pneumonia) if continually fed in a supine position (mortality).

THE GREATEST GOOD

On the other hand, considering the needs or "greatest good" for society means distributing *limited resources* (money for wheelchairs) fairly and to those *most in need*. Limited resources, therefore, should not be allocated in excess to any one individual to the extent that these resources are then not available for others in need. A guiding question for everyone can be

- Can an existing wheelchair or component continue to be used to improve the patient's function, reduce morbidity, or reduce mortality risk?

If the answer is yes, then it behooves the clinician and family to advocate the greatest good of society while still addressing the patient's needs. Unnecessarily ordering wheelchairs or components can result in less funding for others in need, contribute to the national debt of future generations, burden taxpayers, and saturate landfills.

An example is the patient who comes to a clinic wanting a new wheelchair because the existing one is 4 years old. If the wheelchair fits well and addresses the medical and functional needs of the patient, then third-party payers (e.g., Medicaid or Medicare) should not be required to fund a new wheelchair.

INFORMED CONSENT

The patient, family, or caregiver should be made aware of wheelchair recommendations and the rationale for wheelchairs and components before they are ordered. Problems occur when a key figure in the patient's life is not present during the wheelchair evaluation. Benefits, as well as the risks, of not accepting recommendations should be discussed with the patient and family. Alternative wheelchair options should be explored if they are reasonable. If the patient or family does not agree with recommendations, much time and energy is saved by halting the order and paperwork.

REFERENCES

1. Callihan JC. Basics and Background. In JC Callihan (ed), Ethical Issues in Professional Life. New York: Oxford University Press, 1988;3–25.

Why Things Can Go Wrong Even Though You Think You Did Your Job

PATIENT SATISFACTION

If a patient is not satisfied with wheelchair recommendations, it is likely because the patient's expectations of what the wheelchair would do have not been fulfilled. The family may request a wheelchair to solve a problem that it is not capable of solving. Often, there is no medical justification for the requested wheelchair. In other words, it does not improve function, minimize morbidity, or reduce mortality of the patient. The remedy, in hindsight, is clear communication and education. When possible, try to dispel myths that the patient or family may have about wheelchairs.

MYTHS ABOUT WHEELCHAIRS

Myth 1: The Wheelchair Is Old; Therefore, a New One Is Needed

I have seen wheelchairs that are 10 years old and look like new, whereas other wheelchairs are only 1 year old and are ready for the graveyard. Recommendations for a new wheelchair should be based on medical need. Consider a new wheelchair if

- The patient completely outgrew the frame (metal structure).
- The frame is broken and not repairable.
- A different type of wheelchair is medically necessary due to a change in the patient's medical condition.
- The wheelchair is old and had a long and ongoing repair history.

Myth 2: The Wheelchair Is Broken; Therefore, a New One Is Needed

Frequently, when a wheelchair component breaks, it can be replaced much like a part of a car can be replaced. Even when an entire side of the wheelchair frame cracks, it is possible and may be less expensive to replace the side of the wheelchair than to order a new wheelchair.

Myth 3: A New Wheelchair Will Make My Child Better

A wheelchair provides transportation and postural support. It can support the patient to function maximally with existing abilities and can significantly improve postural alignment. It will not, however, cure a disease, straighten a fixed spinal deformity, or guarantee a pressure-sore–free existence.

Myth 4: The Wheelchair Is Self-Cleaning

Wheelchairs are not like self-cleaning ovens. Bugs (e.g., cockroaches) love to live in the hollow tubings of the wheelchair frame. In my experience, manufacturers appear more embarrassed than helpful when the problem of infestation is brought up.

If the patient eats in the wheelchair, the chair should be cleaned after each meal. Upholstery (vinyl) can be cleaned with a damp sponge and soap or mild detergent.[1] The metal frame of the wheelchair should not be hosed down with water, because it may rust and weaken. Instead, consider periodically cleaning the metal frame with wax containing a cleaner (e.g., auto wax).[1]

Myth 5: A Pommel Will Stop the Patient from Sliding Forward

A pommel is a padded block positioned between the patient's knees that is designed to keep the hips in adequate abduction and the knees from pressing together. If the patient slides forward in the wheelchair, the patient will eventually slide into and press against the pommel. Although a pommel may stop the patient from falling completely out of the wheelchair, it could also cause excessive pressure, discomfort, and ulceration to the patient's groin. Furthermore, the patient's position will remain poor because the patient's pelvis will be toward the front edge of the seat rather than properly placed toward the rear of the seat. Please be humane and do not use a pommel for your patient's sliding problems. Identify the cause of the sliding problem and consider alternative ways to solve the problem, such as use of antithrust seats, tilt-in-space frames, sub anterior superior iliac spine bars, peroneal straps, or a different seat belt angle.

Myth 6: A Chest Harness (Anterior Trunk Support) Will Stop Forward Sliding

A chest harness is designed to give anterior trunk support but is not designed to stop a patient's pelvis from sliding forward. In fact, if forward sliding occurs, the patient's neck could become entangled in the top of the chest harness, resulting in death due to asphyxiation.[2] Address the sliding problem by stabilizing the patient's pelvis rather than the trunk.

Myth 7: A Lap Board Will Stop Forward Sliding

The lap board is meant to be a table surface for the patient. If the patient slides forward into a lap board, the rib cage will eventually press against the inside edge of the board, causing unnecessary discomfort and interference with breathing. The lap board will not stop sliding behavior and probably will not prevent the patient from sliding under the board and out of the wheelchair.

Myth 8: The Seat Belt Is Secured Across the Waist

Seat belts should be secured across the hips to stabilize the pelvis (i.e., in the crease between the pelvis and thigh when you raise your knee toward your chest), not across the waist. You would be surprised how many people do not really know the difference between their waist and hips if you ask them to point to their hips. If the seat belt is strapped across the waist (i.e., between the chest and the pelvis), the patient may have enough room to slide underneath the belt.

Myth 9: The Patient Can Sit in the Same Wheelchair Position All Day

It is difficult for anyone to sit in one position for a long period of time. Think of how often you change position in your seat when you see a movie. Patients in wheelchairs are no different. They must adjust their sitting position throughout the day to relieve pressure. Even the best seat cushion (whatever that may be someday) will not prevent a pressure sore from developing unless the patient also periodically relieves pressure under the buttocks. If patients cannot adjust themselves, then someone must do it for them.

Myth 10: Power Mobility Is a Symbol of Further Disability

Power mobility can in fact increase mobility while conserving energies of the user for more productive activities.[3] Individuals who have made the transition to power mobility have reported an improved social and work life.[4]

Myth 11: Ring Cushions and Donut-Type Devices Are Good for Relieving Pressure While Sitting

Ring or donut-type cushions may actually be deleterious in terms of pressure-sore development since these devices have been shown to increase venous congestion.[5]

I am always amazed to see how frequently these ring cushions are still being prescribed or bought.

REFERENCES

1. Wheelchair Prescription: Care and Service (booklet no. 4). Los Angeles: Everest & Jennings, 1976;10–16.
2. Rubin BS, Dube AH, Mitchell EK. Asphyxial deaths due to physical restraint: a case series. Arch Fam Med 1993;2:405–408.
3. Warren CG. Technical considerations: power mobility and its implications. J Rehabil Res Dev 1990;2(suppl):44–85.
4. Miles-Tapping C, MacDonald LJ. Lifestyle implications of power mobility. Phys Occup Ther Geriatr 1994;12:31–49.
5. Panel for the Prediction and Prevention of Pressure Ulcers in Adults. Pressure Ulcers in Adults: Prediction and Prevention. Clinical Practice Guideline, no. 3. AHCPR pub. no. 92-0047. Rockville, MD: Agency for Health Care Policy and Research, Public Health Service, U.S. Department of Health and Human Services, 1992;26.

A3

General Body Shape

Body shape needs to be considered for a proper wheel-chair fit just as one would consider sleeve length and neck size for a proper shirt fit.

Diversity is normal. Human beings do not all look the same: It would be a very boring world if everyone did look alike. When a patient does not fit well in a wheel-chair, it may be because the patient's *unique body shape* was not taken into consideration. Small variations in a patient's shape can make a huge difference in how the patient fits and feels in the wheelchair.

TYPES OF BODY SHAPES

People can generally be described in terms of being pre-dominately *round*, *muscular*, or *fragile* (i.e., endomorphy, mesomorphy, or ectomorphy) (Figure A3.1).[1]

- Endomorphy: round
- Mesomorphy: muscular
- Ectomorphy: fragile

Extreme round shapes are seen in sumo wrestlers and are characterized by round, soft, smooth contours. Extreme

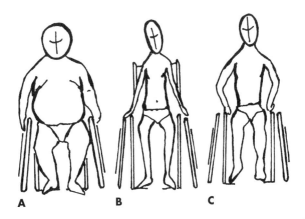

Fig. A3.1 Body types. A. Endomorphs have round shapes. B. Ectomorphs have linear, fragile shapes. C. Mesomorphs have muscular shapes.

muscular shapes are seen in the beach bullies who kick sand in your face and are characterized by square, hard, massive contours. Finally, extreme fragile shapes are seen in the beach weaklings who have the sand kicked in their faces. Fragile shapes are characterized by thin bodies and delicate contours. Actually, everyone has elements of all three components (i.e., round, fragile, muscular) in them.

When you look at a patient, it may be helpful to describe their physique in terms of these three body shapes. For example, the patient with quadriplegia may have a round belly, fragile chest, fragile limbs, and muscular neck. The patient with paraplegia may have fragile legs, muscular arms, a muscular chest, and very little roundness. A third patient with obesity may have round and soft arms, trunk, and legs and very little muscular definition. Because no two people have the same body shape, no two people have the same exact fit in a wheelchair. Different body shapes require varying amounts of wheelchair space.

AGE AND BODY SHAPE

Body size and proportions (i.e., relative size of body parts) change dramatically from infancy to adulthood. Children, for example, expand with age, whereas the elderly, on the other hand, tend to shrink. In addition, the head size of an infant is 25% of body size, whereas in an adult, head size is 12.5% of body size.[2] It is therefore important to account for the patient's age when fitting a patient to a wheelchair.

Infants

- Relatively large heads
- Long trunks
- Short lower limbs
- Rounded spines

Childhood

- Thighs and forearms show growth
- Spine develops the four curves or arches

Puberty

Girls begin to exhibit

- Curvilinear shape
- Increased breast size
- Increased pelvic growth
- Greater local fat deposit

In both sexes, the lumbar arch becomes more prominent.

Mature Adult

- Increased weight gain may be noted.

Elderly

- Shorter trunk stature (due to loss of water in the vertebral disks)[2]

GENDER AND BODY SHAPE

The body shapes of males and females begin to show differences at puberty. Bone and fat distribution account for much of the shape variations between men and women and should be considered when fitting patients in wheelchairs.

Women

Bone Dimensions

In general, compared to men, women have the following:

- Wider hips
- Longer trunk length
- Greater chest depth
- Shorter upper limbs (due to shorter humerus)
- Higher relative elbow height
- Shorter collar bone
- Narrower shoulder width
- Relatively shorter thigh (due to the shorter femur)
- Deeper and wider pelvis
- Wider hip position
- Shorter and narrower foot

Fatty Tissue

Fatty tissue is more evident in the trunk than the limbs, with women tending to have more fat than men. In women, fat deposits can be noted at the following:

- Vertebra prominence (base of the neck)
- Posterior deltoid fat (back of the upper arm)
- Mammary fat (the breast)
- Flank fat (the sides of the trunk)
- Gluteal fat (buttocks)
- Subtrochanter fat (outside of the thigh)
- Abdominal fat (belly below the navel)

Men

Men, on the other hand, tend to deposit fat in the abdomen *above the navel.* In addition, whereas the widest portion of the lower limb tends to be at the hip level (trochanter) in men, in women the widest area is lower, at the subtrochanter level.

Differences in physical characteristics between men and women are not as clear-cut as one might think. Consider each individual as falling somewhere within a continuum between having strong male characteristics and having strong female characteristics.[3]

WEIGHTBEARING AND BODY SHAPE

The shape of a body part changes when it presses against a firm surface. Be aware that the patient may need more room in the wheelchair as a result of spreading flesh (soft tissue) (Figure A3.2).

MOVEMENTS AND BODY SHAPE

Body parts change shape as the patient moves. The hamstring muscle, for example, may fit well on a seat when relaxed but may dig into the front edge of the seat due to shape changes when tensed.

CLOTHING AND BODY SHAPE

Clothes can affect how the patient fits in the wheelchair since clothing tends to alter the external shape of an individual. Imagine, during the 1800s, trying to fit a female patient in a wheelchair who insists on wearing a hoop skirt (i.e., cage crinoline) undergarment made of steel.[4] If a patient has eccentric taste in clothing, he or she should

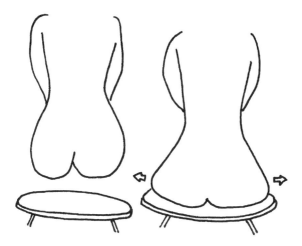

Fig. A3.2 A patient may require additional seat width due to soft tissue compression.

wear the clothing on the day of the clinic visit so that the clothing can be accommodated in the wheelchair. Also note that some clothing may have a slippery quality (i.e., low friction coefficient) that may cause the patient to slide forward in his or her wheelchair.

HAIRSTYLES AND BODY SHAPE

Hair can be viewed as an extension of a person's body. Hairstyle is only a problem if the patient needs a headrest, and the hair gathering behind the head interferes with contact points on the headrest. An example would be someone who wears a bouffant hairstyle of the 1960s.[4] Hats with brims can also be a problem for the same reason.

ORTHOPEDIC DEVICES AND BODY SHAPE

Body jackets and braces take up space in the patient's wheelchair. A body jacket tends to push the patient forward and widen the patient in the wheelchair. As a result, the wheelchair seat appears to be short and narrow. Try to anticipate if the patient will be using orthopedic devices in the wheelchair so you can plan for the additional room.

REFERENCES

1. Sheldon WH. The Varieties of Human Physique: An Introduction to Constitution Psychology. New York: Harper and Brothers, 1940;1–9.
2. Peck SR. Atlas of Human Anatomy for the Artist. Oxford, UK: Oxford University Press, 1982;215.
3. Downs JF, Bleibtreu HK. Human Variation: An Introduction to Physical Anthropology (rev ed). Beverly Hills, CA: Glencoe Press, 1972;295–316.
4. Tortora P, Eubank K. Survey of Historic Costume: A History of Western Dress (2nd ed). New York: Fairchild Publications, 1994;304–305, 424–425.

A4

Local Body Shape: The Missing Piece in the Evaluation

Determine how much space each body part will occupy in the wheelchair (Figure A4.1).

HEAD

Shape

- Head shape may be predominately large, round, spherical, cubical, or irregular.
- The back of the head may be curved or flat (where the head and neck meet).
- Ears may be large or small, projected out to the side (laterally), or flat; ears may also be located at different heights on the sides of the head. In young children, ears may be more round.[1]
- Note the proximity of the ear to the temporomandibular joint on each side of the head.

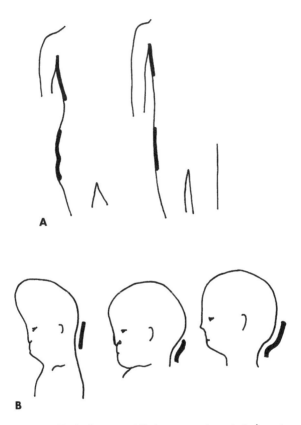

Fig. A4.1 Local body shape can differ between patients. A. Body contours at the chest and hip differ between men and women and may require different amounts of space in the seating system. B. Head shapes may vary and require different amounts of head support in the occipital area.

Function

- The head carries the special senses (i.e., hearing and vision) that enable an individual to interact with his or her surroundings.
- Head position influences the distribution of muscle tonus in the extremities.[2]

Implication for the Wheelchair

- Wheelchair components that affect head position (e.g., headrests, neck rings, head bands) can interfere with the patient's ability to orient his or her head and affect muscle tonus in the body.

NECK

Shape

The neck can be predominately

- Short
- Long and wide laterally
- Long and slender
- Apparently absent (i.e., hidden under elevated scapula)

Function

The neck provides the following:

- Joint mobility
- Muscular stability

- The passageway for oxygen, nutrients, blood, and nerve supply to the head

Implications for the Wheelchair

- Wheelchair components should not interfere with neck mobility or compress vascular, neural, or airway structures in the neck.
- Because of the risk of strangulation, chest harnesses should be used only if necessary, with adequate supervision, and at a safe distance from the patient's neck.[3]

SCAPULAE

Function

The scapulae participate in a rhythm during arm reaching movements by gliding over the rib cage.[4] Place your right hand over your left scapula and notice how it slides as your left arm reaches forward. If the scapulae are prevented from sliding, the individual cannot attain a full upper extremity reach.

Implications for the Wheelchair

Wheelchair components should not interfere with scapula movements during reaching and self-propulsion.

- If an anterior trunk support strap is too tightly secured over the shoulders (i.e., crossing the clavicle), it can interfere with scapulae movements in patients who have functional use of their arms. This is particularly important during overhead reaching activities.

- If the back insert of the wheelchair is too high, it can interfere with scapulae movements (i.e., adduction, depression) associated with backward arm movements during wheelchair propulsion.

UPPER LIMBS

Shape

The limbs can be predominately

- Short and tapered
- Massive and muscular
- Long and slender

Function

The upper limb has the special function of propulsion for wheelchair users.

Implications for the Wheelchair

Position rear wheels optimally to maximize upper extremity reach and propulsion efficiency.

GENERAL TRUNK SHAPES

General trunk shape helps determine space requirements in the wheelchair.

- The chest mass may predominate over the abdomen mass.
- The abdominal mass may predominate over the chest mass.
- The shape may be linear (i.e., chest and abdomen are approximately equal in mass).

UPPER TRUNK

Shape

The upper trunk is characterized by varying amounts of muscle tissue and breast tissue.

- Breast tissue in either gender is oriented forward and to the side rather than directly forward. The ribcage shape appears to slope downward and medially due to soft tissue coverage (i.e., latissimus dorsi). In the emaciated patient, however, soft tissue is lost and the ribcage can be seen to flair out laterally and take on the appearance of a lamp shade.[1]
- The upper spine may appear mildly rounded (normal), flat, very rounded (kyphosis), or crooked (scoliosis).
- Note that the sides of the trunk are curved rather than square in shape.

Function

The upper trunk houses and protects the vital organs (i.e., heart, lungs); permits joint mobility, such as rotation; and changes volume (i.e., costal excursion) during breathing.

Implications for the Wheelchair

Wheelchair components, such as lateral trunk supports and anterior trunk supports, should not be so tight against the skin that they impede costal excursion and breathing.

- If the patient possesses large amounts of breast tissue but requires anterior trunk support, then a harness that accommodates the shape of the breast tissue may need to be considered.
- If the patient has the ability to functionally rotate the upper trunk, then reconsider wheelchair components that may interfere with the patient's ability to rotate (i.e., high back inserts, chest straps, and harnesses).
- If the patient has a marked, fixed scoliosis, then a molded back insert may be needed to accommodate spinal convexities and concavities.
- If the patient has a fixed kyphosis, then a curved back insert (i.e., shaped like a spoon) may be necessary to provide pressure relief for the symmetric hump.
- Curved lateral trunk supports provide greater pressure distribution than planar-shaped supports.

PELVIS

The pelvis is the key to good positioning and the first thing one evaluates. The shape of the low back (as well as the upper trunk, upper limbs, lower limbs, and head) is often determined by the position of the pelvis. The pelvis is so important that more information follows.

Shape

The low back can be mildly arched (normal), very arched (lordosis), flat, very rounded (kyphosis), or crooked (scoliosis).

Function

The pelvis is the base of support for sitting. The pelvis must act as a stable foundation for upper body activities involving the trunk, arms, and head.

Three Planes of Movement

Imagine the pelvis as a bowl. Like a bowl, the pelvis can be moved in three different planes.[5]

1. Tilted (anteriorly or posteriorly) in the sagittal plane
2. Obliquely (elevated or depressed on one side) in the coronal plane
3. Rotated (in the transverse plane)

Implications for the Wheelchair

- The pelvic position determines how the patient sits. Ideally, you want the pelvis to be supported in a *neutral position* so that the patient can sit properly and function maximally. In the neutral position, there is no extreme tilting, raising, or twisting of the pelvis in any direction; a natural arch is noted in the small of the back; and weight is equally distributed under the ischia.

- Please note, however, that sitting is not normally a static activity. Pelvic movement does occur during functional activities and to relieve pressure under the buttocks.
- If the pelvis is not supported in a neutral position, kyphotic, lordotic, pelvic obliquity, or pelvic rotational deformity can result.

The Neutral Pelvic Position

- The pelvis is not excessively tilted anteriorly or posteriorly (i.e., allows for a small natural arch in the low back), with weightbearing over the ischia.
- The anterior superior iliac spines (ASISs) are on a level plane so that there is equal distribution of weight over each ischium.
- The ASISs are facing front so that one ASIS is not rotated forward more than the other one.

Posterior Pelvic Tilt

- If the pelvis is tilted backward excessively, the low back tends to round; excessive pressure on the sacrum and coccyx, labored breathing, and difficulty reaching forward can result.

Anterior Pelvic Tilt

- If the pelvis is tilted anteriorly excessively, the low back may appear arched, and excessive pressure under the thighs, discomfort, and fatigue may result.

Pelvic Obliquity

- If the pelvis is elevated on one side and depressed on the other side, there may be excessive pressure under the ischia of the depressed side, which can result in a pressure sore.

Pelvic Rotation

- If the pelvis is rotated anteriorly on one side and rotated backward on the other, the lower extremities may become windswept or the individual's face may orient toward the side rather than to the front.

LOWER LIMBS

Function

The lower limbs were designed for locomotion. In a wheelchair, the lower limbs may still be able to participate in wheelchair locomotion if the feet can reach the ground.

Implications for the Wheelchair

- If the patient cannot use the upper extremities well but has potential to use his or her lower extremities, the wheelchair frame should be low enough to the ground to allow foot-assisted propulsion. Make sure there is adequate space between the back of the knee and the front of the seat to permit knee flexion during foot propulsion.

- Nerve sites that control lower limb movements are susceptible to injury from pressure. These areas include the popliteal fossa (posterior tibial nerve) and the fibula head (common peroneal nerve). Avoid excessive pressure from wheelchair components at these nerve sites.

EXERCISES

Please note: Only do movements that are comfortable and not medically contraindicated. Breathe normally and avoid straining.

Body Shape Changes with Movement

Note how body shape is affected by movement, tension, compression, and respirations. Use a tape measure to record changes in width or thickness of body parts.

1. Note how the foot changes shape and spreads out when you stand and place weight on it.
2. Note how your thigh widens and takes up more space when you sit on a firm surface.
3. Stand behind a friend and note how much the buttock area (soft tissue) spreads in width as he or she sits down on a stool. Look at this phenomenon with other friends of different body types when they sit on firm versus sling-type seats.
4. Breathing is a perfect example of how the body changes shape during movement. Notice how your

chest widens *in all directions* and your abdomen expands forward and to the sides as you inhale.

5. Notice how your rib cage on the right side rounds in shape as you reach to the ceiling with your right arm.
6. Notice how the arch in the small of your back disappears as you reach for the floor. (Place one hand in the small of your back to sense the change.)
7. Finally, notice how your biceps muscle changes shape and appears to become taller as you tense your upper arm.

Pelvic Position Affects Body Shape

Feel how the position of the pelvis affects your body shape by performing the following pelvic movements gently. Sit on a stool or firm chair with your feet on the floor.

1. First, find your neutral sitting position, where you may notice a small hollow space in the small of your back. (Place your hand in the small of your back and feel it.) In this position, you are placing the same amount of weight on both sides of your body. (Please note that there is a lot of variation in how people sit. Do what is comfortable.)
2. Tilt your pelvis backward by rounding your back and looking at your navel. Notice how the natural hollow area in the small of your back disappears. Notice how you tend to shorten in height and sit on your sacrum while in this position. Also notice how much more difficult it is to breathe and reach forward from this position. (This is how *many* patients sit in wheelchairs.)

3. Tilt your pelvis forward by arching your back and looking up toward the ceiling. Notice how the natural hollow space in the small of your back becomes larger. Also notice how you would have to strain to maintain this position for a long duration.

4. Elevate your left pelvis by raising your left hip up off the seat while you shift your weight over to your right side. Notice how this position places greater weight under your right ischium and that you would become very uncomfortable if you maintained this posture over a period of time.

5. Rotate your pelvis by gently moving only your left hip closer to the front edge of the seat while keeping your right hip stationary. Notice how this sitting position tends to twist your body to the right side and out of midline.

REFERENCES

1. Peck SR. Atlas of Human Anatomy for the Artist. Oxford, UK: Oxford University Press, 1982;167, 178.
2. Fiorentino MR. Reflex Testing Methods For Evaluating CNS Development (2nd ed). Springfield, IL: Thomas, 1981;13.
3. Rubin BS, Dube AH, Mitchell EK. Asphyxial deaths due to physical restraint: a case series. Arch Fam Med 1993;2:405–408.
4. Cailliet R. Shoulder Pain. Philadelphia: Davis, 1991;42–46.
5. Currie DM, Hardwick K, Marburger RA, Britell CW. Wheelchair Prescription and Adaptive Seating. In JL Delisa, BM Gans (eds), Rehabilitation Medicine: Principles and Practice (2nd ed). Philadelphia: Lippincott, 1993;574.

Seven Skills to Teach the Caregiver

1: TEACH PROPER POSITIONING IN THE WHEELCHAIR

Proper positioning cannot be emphasized enough. No wheelchair can be good if the patient is not placed into the wheelchair properly.

- Step 1: Lock the wheel locks on the wheelchair.
- Step 2: Transfer the patient into the wheelchair.
- Step 3: Move the patient's pelvis back into the rear of the seat until the back of the pelvis touches the back insert of the wheelchair. (This is not as easy as it sounds.) Confirm that the patient's pelvis is back in the seat by gently leaning the patient's trunk forward (if possible) and then checking that there is no gap (space) between the back of the pelvis and the back insert of the wheelchair.
- Step 4: Secure the seat belt across the patient's hips firmly (so that you can only fit approximately the width of two fingers between the seat belt and the

patient's body). The patient's pelvis must be maintained back in the seat while you secure the seat belt.

2: TEACH HOW WHEELCHAIR COMPONENTS OPERATE

Each company designs its components a little differently. I remember scratching my head for 10 minutes before figuring out how to remove a high-tech armrest.

Having the caregivers physically operate each component during the clinic visit may help them to remember the procedures later.

- Wheel locks
- Seat belt
- Armrests
- Front rigging
- Anti-tippers
- Removal of inserts
- Proper use of straps, anterior trunk supports, and positioning blocks

3: TEACH HOW THE WHEELCHAIR FOLDS

About once a month, I run into a family who has owned a wheelchair for several years yet never knew it could fold. Folding a wheelchair can allow it to fit in a car so that the family can go on a trip. Usually, seat and back inserts must be removed first before the frame can fold. Caution caregivers about catching their fingers between the rails while unfolding the frame.

4: TEACH WHEELCHAIR CLEANING[1, 2]

- Most wheelchair components can be cleaned using warm water and mild soap.
- Naugahyde should be cleaned with warm water and mild soap.
- Metal parts should be cleaned with a wax with a cleaner (i.e., auto wax).
- Avoid dripping liquid into openings of metal parts.
- Wood, leather, and leatherette should be cleaned with upholstery wax.
- Completely dry all components.

5: TEACH WHEELCHAIR MAINTENANCE

Wheelchair parts tend to loosen with time. Tightening loose nuts helps prevent the later loss of parts. Have the caregiver check the wheelchair periodically. If a part falls off and the caregiver or patient is not sure how it reattaches, instruct them to put it in a "wheelchair parts box" (shoe box or bag) and ask the durable medical equipment dealer or clinic to reinstall the part as soon as possible.

6: TEACH THE CAREGIVER TO SAFELY NEGOTIATE CURBS, RAMPS, AND STEPS WITH THE WHEELCHAIR

7: TEACH THE CAREGIVER TO USE PROPER BODY MECHANICS DURING PATIENT LIFTS AND TRANSFERS

REFERENCES

1. Kamenetz HL. The Wheelchair Book: Mobility for the Disabled. Springfield, IL: Thomas, 1969;198–207.
2. Wheelchair Prescription: Care and Service (booklet no. 4). Los Angeles: Everest & Jennings, 1976;6–16.

A6

Product Directory of Manufacturers and Suppliers of Wheelchairs and Seat Cushions*

MANUAL WHEELCHAIRS

Abbey Home Healthcare
3560 Hyland Ave.
Costa Mesa, CA 92626-1438
1-714-957-2000

Adaptive Driving Systems, Inc.
21050 Superior St.
Chatsworth, CA 91311-4321
1-818-998-1026

ADC Services
15 W. Fullerton Ave.
Addison, IL 60101-4648
1-708-832-0203

Al's Woodcraft, Inc.
435 E. Main St.
Borden, IN 47106
1-800-872-6426

Alan's Wheelchairs & Repairs
2060 Emery Ave. #204
La Habra, CA 90631-5773
1-714-639-8222

Alco Sales & Service Co.
6851 High Grove Blvd.
Burr Ridge, IL 60521
1-800-323-4282

*Medical Device Register. The Official Directory of Medical Suppliers (Vol. 1, sec. 111). Montvale, NJ: Medical Economics, 1996;358–359; 1192–1195.

American Bantex
1640 Rollins Rd.
Burlingame, CA 94011-4098
1-800-633-4839

American Marketing Associates
10733 E. Bethany Dr.
Aurora, CO 80014-2603
1-800-262-6407

Anthony Brothers MFG
1945 S. Rancho Santa Fe Rd.
San Marcos, CA 92069-5124
1-619-744-4763

Armstrong Medical
Industries, Inc.
575 Knightsbridge Pkwy.
Lincolnshire, IL 60069-0700
1-800-323-4220

ATD-American Co.,
Patient Aid Div.
135 Greenwood Ave.
Wyncote, PA 19095-1337
1-800-523-2300

Bowers Co.
430 E. Pacific Coast Hwy.
Long Beach, CA 90806-6219
1-800-537-0505

Brownstone Trading Co.
714 E. University
El Paso, TX 79902
1-915-542-0240

C.R. Newton Co., LTD
1575 S. Beretania St., Suite 101
Honolulu, HI 96826-1141
1-800-545-2078

C.F. Wood Industries
7021 W. Augusta, Suite 108
Glendale, AZ 85303-1206
1-602-939-0570

Camtec, Cambridge
Technologies, Inc.
300 Muir St.
Cambridge, MD 21613-1819
1-800-866-1156

Canyon Products
10173 Croydon Way, Suite 1
Sacramento, CA 95827-2108
1-800-221-5499

Care Catalog Services
1877 N.E. 7th Ave.
Portland, OR 97212-3905
1-800-443-7091

Central New York
Medical Products
749 W. Genesee St.
Syracuse, NY 13204
1-315-428-9945

Convaid Products, Inc.
P.O. Box 4209
Rancho Palos Verdes, CA
90274-9579
1-800-552-1020

Dalton Medical Corp.
Box 833065
Richardson, TX 75083-3065
1-214-418-2447

Damaco, Inc.
5105 Maureen Lane
Moorpark, CA 93021
1-800-432-2434

Diller Medical, Inc.
902 N. Main St.
Bluffton, OH 45817
1-800-537-1900

Eagle Sports Chairs
2351 Parkwood Rd.
Snellville, GA 30278-4003
1-800-932-9380

ETAC USA
2325 Parklawn Rd., Suite J
Waukesha, WI 53186-2938
1-800-678-3822

Everest & Jennings Intl.
4203 Earth City Expressway
Earth City, MO 63048-1304
1-800-235-4661

Five Star Mobility
P.O. Box 1540
Matthews, NC 28106
1-800-833-9962

Freedom Designs, Inc.
2241 Madera Rd.
Simi Valley, CA 93065
1-800-331-8551

Gendron, Inc.
Lugbill Rd.
Archbold, OH 43502-0197
1-800-537-2521

Giant Lift Equipment
Mfg. Co., Inc.
136 Lafayette Rd.
North Hampton, NH 03862
1-800-524-4268

Goldsouth Medical
2136 Stagecoach Rd.
Stockton, CA 95205-9001
1-800-366-0221

Graham-Field, Inc.
400 Rabro Dr. E.
Hauppauge, NY 11788-4226
1-800-645-8176

Guardian Products, Inc.
4175 Guardian St.
Simi Valley, CA 93063
1-800-423-8034

Harvy Surgical Supply Corp.
34–35 Collins Pl.
Flushing, NY 11354-2790
1-800-221-0142

Idea, Inc.
1393 Meadowcreek Dr., #2
Pewaukee, WI 53072-3926
1-414-691-4248

Ideal Medical Services Co.
9203 Zake Rd.
Houston, TX 77064
1-800-336-8020

Innovative Concepts
300 N. State St.
Girard, OH 44420
1-800-676-5030

International Healthcare
Solutions, Inc.
368 Veterans Memorial Hwy.
Commack, NY 11725
1-800-791-0932

Invacare Corp.
899 Cleveland St.
Elyria, OH 44036-2125
1-800-333-6900

Iron Horse Productions, Inc.
2624 Conner
Port Huron, MI 48060-6965
1-800-426-0354

J.J. Balan, Inc.
5725 Foster Ave.
Brooklyn, NY 11234-1001
1-800-552-2526

Jaken Medical
2346 E. Walnut Ave.
Fullerton, CA 92631
1-800-678-4499

Kareco International, Inc.
299 Rte. 22 E.
Green Brook, NJ 08812-1714
1-800-8KARECO

Karman Healthcare, Inc.
9662 E. Rush St.
South El Monte, CA 91733
1-818-279-7628

Kendall-Futuro Co.
5405 Dupont Circle, Suite A
Milford, OH 45150
1-513-576-8000

Labac Systems
3535 S. Kipling St.
Lakewood, CO 80235
1-800-445-4402

Lemans Industries Corp.
79 Express St.
Plainview, NY 11803-2404
1-800-289-5667

Lincare, Inc.
P.O. Box 9004
Clearwater, FL 34618-9004
1-800-284-2006

Lumex
81 Spence St.
Bay Shore, NY 11706-2231
1-800-645-5272

McKesson Home Health Care
One Post St.
San Francisco, CA 94104-5201
1-800-634-1164

Med Group, Inc.
3223 S. Loop 289, Suite 600
Lubbock, TX 79423-1331
1-800-825-5633

Medi-Products
500 Glenbrook Rd.
Stamford, CT 06906-1821
1-800-765-3237

Medical Supplies of America,
Inc., DBA Medapex
P.O. Box 915
Tucker, GA 30085-0915
1-800-347-5678

Metro Medical
1911 Church St.
Nashville, TN 37203-2203
1-800-277-7724

Mulholland Positioning
Systems, Inc.
215 N. 12th St.
Santa Paula, CA 93060-2917
1-800-543-4769

National Medical Excess Corp.
144 E. Kingsbridge Rd.
Mount Vernon, NY 10550
1-800-872-5407

North American Medical
Specialties
7021 W. Augusta, Suite 108
Glendale, AZ 85303-1206
1-602-939-0570

Ocelco, Inc.
1111 Industrial Park Rd.
Brainerd, MN 56401
1-800-328-5343

Omni Manufacturing, Inc.
2935 Bankers Industrial Dr.
Atlanta, GA 30360
1-800-849-6664

Ortho-Kinetics, Inc.
West 220 N. 507 Springdale Rd.
Waukesha, WI 53186
1-800-446-4522

Palmer Industries
P.O. Box 5707, Union Station
Endicott, NY 13760-0988
1-800-847-1304

Permobil
6B Gill St.
Woburn, MA 01801
1-800-736-0925

Phil Wood & Company
580 N. 6th St.
San Jose, CA 95112-3237
1-408-298-1540

PSP Medical Rentals & Sales
11731 E. Telegraph Rd., Suite K
Santa Fe Springs, CA 90670
1-800-841-0101

Quickie Designs, Inc.
2842 Business Park Ave.
Fresno, CA 93727-1328
1-800-456-8168

Red Line Healthcare
8121 10th Ave. N.
Golden Valley, MN 55427-4401
1-800-328-8111

Redman Wheelchairs
945 E. Ohio St., # 4
Tucson, AZ 85714-1694
1-800-727-6684

Respiratory Services, Inc.
524 Broad St.
Gadsden, AL 35901-3720
1-800-264-0062

Rx Rocker Corp.
3541 Old Conejo Rd., Suite 101
Newbury Park, CA 91320-2158
1-800-762-5371

Samhall, Inc.
300 Long Beach Blvd.
Stratford, CT 06497-7153
1-800-882-0098

Sammons-Preston, Inc.
4 Sammons Ct.
Brook, IL 60440-5071
1-800-323-5547

Savant Medical
1215 S. Harlem
Forest Park, IL 60130-2407
1-708-771-2000

Snug Seat, Inc.
10810 Independence Point Pkwy.
Matthews, NC 28106-1739
1-800-336-7684

SSC Medical Products
P.O. Box 48329
Atlanta, GA 30362
1-800-874-2692

Stryker Corp., Medical Div.
6300 Sprinkle Rd.
Kalamazoo, MI 49001-8701
1-800-669-4968

Sunrise Medical, Inc.
2382 Faraday Ave., Suite 200
Carlsbad, CA 92008
1-619-930-1500

Theradyne Corp.
21730 Hanover Ave.
Lakeville, MN 55044-9108
1-800-328-4014

Tuffcare, Inc.
3998 E. La Palma
Anaheim, CA 92807
1-800-367-6160

Wheel Ring, Inc.
199 Forest St.
Manchester, CT 06040-5980
1-203-647-8596

Wheelchair Sales and
Service Co., Inc.
315 Main St.
West Springfield, MA 01090
1-413-736-0376

Wheelchairs of Kansas
204 W. 2nd St.
Ellis, KS 67548
1-800-537-6454

Youngs, Inc.
55 Cherry Ln.
Souderton, PA 18964-1550
1-800-523-5454

POWERED WHEELCHAIRS

Abbey Home Healthcare
3560 Hyland Ave.
Costa Mesa, CA 92626-1438
1-714-957-2000

Alan's Wheelchairs & Repairs
2060 Emery Ave., #204
La Habra, CA 90631-5773
1-714-639-8222

Cliffcor Medical
1211–1215 Mishawaka Ave.
South Bend, IN 46615-1127
1-219-233-7918

Curtis Instruments, Inc.
200 Kisco Ave.
Mount Kisco, NY 10549
1-914-666-2971

Damaco, Inc.
5105 Maureen Ln.
Moorpark, CA 93021
1-800-432-2434

Everest & Jennings Intl.
4203 Earth City Expressway
Earth City, MO 63048-1304
1-800-235-4661

International Healthcare
Solutions, Inc.
368 Veterans Memorial Hwy.
Commack, NY 11725
1-800-791-0932

Invacare Corp.
899 Cleveland St.
Elyria, OH 44036-2125
1-800-333-6900

Kempf
1080 E. Duane Ave., #E
Sunnyvale, CA 94086-2628
1-800-255-6174

Med Group, Inc.
3223 S. Loop 289, Suite 600
Lubbock, TX 79423-1331
1-800-825-5633

Medi-Products
500 Glenbrook Rd.
Stamford, CT 06906-1821
1-800-765-3237

Medical Supplies of America,
Inc., DBA
Medapex
P.O. Box 915
Tucker, GA 30085-0915
1-800-347-5678

Missouri Stairway Lift Corp.
601 N. College Ave.
Columbia, MO 65201-4770
1-800-392-2591

Mobilchair Corp.
8250 Vickers St., Suite D
San Diego, CA 92111-2117
1-619-292-4865

Mobilectrics
4014 Bardstown Rd.
Louisville, KY 40218
1-800-876-6846

Motovator
1732 Border Ave.
Torrance, CA 90501-3601
1-800-435-2721

Ocelco, Inc.
1111 Industrial Park Rd.
Brainerd, MN 56401
1-800-328-5343

Palmer Industries
P.O. Box 5707, Union Station
Endicott, NY 13760-0988
1-800-847-1304

Permobil
6B Gill St.
Woburn, MA 01801
1-800-736-0925

Pride Health Care, Inc.
182 Susquehanna Ave.
Exeter, PA 18643
1-800-800-8586

Quickie Designs, Inc.
2842 Business Park Ave.
Fresno, CA 93727-1328
1-800-456-8168

R.C. Sales and Manufacturing
14726 Wake St. N.E.
Ham Lake, MN 55304
1-612-786-6504

Redman Wheelchairs
945 E. Ohio St., #4
Tucson, AZ 85714-1694
1-800-727-6684

Rolcontrol Products Co., Inc.
6700 Worthway
Camarillo, CA 93012-8241
1-800-281-7791

Sears Home Health Care
Products
3333 Beverly Rd.
Hoffman Estates, IL 60179
1-708-875-2500

Sunrise Medical, Inc.
2382 Faraday Ave., Suite 200
Carlsbad, CA 92008
1-619-930-1500

Theradyne Corp.
21730 Hanover Ave.
Lakeville, MN 55044-9108
1-800-328-4014

Therafin Corp.
19747 Wolf Rd.
Mokena, IL 60448-0848
1-800-843-7234

Wheelchair Sales and
Service Co., Inc.
315 Main St.
West Springfield, MA 01090
1-413-736-0376

Wheelchairs of Kansas
204 W. 2nd St.
Ellis, KS 67548
1-800-537-6454

World Class Motor Specialists
9920 Painter Ave.
Santa Fe Springs, CA 90670
1-800-359-1892

STANDUP WHEELCHAIRS

Davismade, Inc.
5242 Roscommon
Burton, MI 48509
1-810-742-0581

Imex Healthcare, Inc.
132 Bell Glen Way
Los Gatos, CA 95032
1-408-358-6320

Kuschall of America
708 Via Alondra
Camarillo, CA 93012-8713
1-800-654-4768

LDC Corporation of America
780 B2 Primos Ave.
Folcroft, PA 19032-2111
1-800-782-6324

MDF Technologies, Inc.
780 B2 Primos Ave.
Folcroft, PA 19032-0153
1-800-448-3159

Med Group, Inc.
3223 S. Loop 289, Suite 600
Lubbock, TX 79423-1331
1-800-825-5633

Midland Manufacturing Co., Inc.
802 Universal Dr.
Columbia, SC 29209
1-803-776-5398

SCOOTER (MOTORIZED THREE-WHEELED VEHICLES)

Amigo Mobility International
6693 Dixie Hwy.
Bridgeport, MI 48722-0402
1-800-821-2710

Anthony Brothers Mfg.
1945 S. Rancho Santa Fe Rd.
San Marcos, CA 92069-5124
1-619-744-4763

Bruno Independent
Living Aids, Inc.
1780 Executive Dr.
Oconomowoc, WI 53066-3932
1-800-882-8183

Burke, Inc.
1800 Marriam Ln.
Kansas City, KS 66106-4714
1-800-255-4147

Complete Mobility Systems, Inc.
1915 W. County Rd. C
Roseville, MN 55113-1320
1-800-788-7479

Electric Mobility Corp.
1 Mobility Plaza
Sewell, NJ 08080
1-800-662-4548

Healthcall Corp.
728 N. 7th St.
Milwaukee, WI 53233
1-800-558-7130

Hoveround
2151 Whitfield Industrial Way
Sarasota, FL 34243
1-800-964-6837

Invacare Corp.
899 Cleveland St.
Elyria, OH 44036-2125
1-800-333-6900

Med Group, Inc.
3223 S. Loop 289, Suite 600
Lubbock, TX 79423-1331
1-8000-825-5633

Ortho-Kinetics, Inc.
West 220 N. 507 Springdale Rd.
Waukesha, WI 53186
1-800-446-4522

Pillar Technology, Inc.
1101 Illinois St.
Neodesha, KS 66757
1-800-621-5258

Pride Health Care, Inc.
182 Susquehanna Ave.
Exeter, PA 18643
1-800-800-8586

Ranger All Season Corp.
P.O. Box 132
George, IA 51237
1-800-225-3811

Stoneheart, Inc.
1921 First St.
Cheney, WA 99004-0329
1-800-572-5783

Sunrise Medical, Inc.
2382 Faraday Ave., Suite 200
Carlsbad, CA 92008
1-619-930-1500

Wheelchair Sales and
Service Co., Inc.
315 Main St.
West Springfield, MA 01090
1-413-736-0376

SEAT CUSHIONS

Abbey Home Healthcare
3560 Hyland Ave.
Costa Mesa, CA 92626-1438
1-714-957-2000

Activeaid, Inc.
One Activeaid Rd.
Redwood Falls, MN 56283-0359
1-800-533-5330

Adaptive Engineering Lab, Inc.
P.O. Box 66
Mukilteo, WA 98275-0066
1-800-327-6080

Adaptive Technologies
2023 Romig Rd.
Akron, OH 44320-3819
1-800-589-2630

Alex Orthopedic, Inc.
1174 North Great Southwest
Parkway, Suite 10
Grand Prairie, TX 75050
1-800-544-2539

Alimed, Inc.
297 High St.
Dedham, MA 02026-2844
1-800-225-2610

Alpha Pro Tech, Inc.
903 W. Center St.
Bldg. E,
Salt Lake, UT 84054-2900
1-800-527-7689

American Health Systems
P.O. Box 26688
Greenville, SC 29616-1688
1-800-234-6655

Better Sleep, Inc.
80 Industrial Rd.
Berkeley Heights, NJ 07922-1532
1-908-464-2200

Bio Clinic Corp.
4083 E. Airport Dr.
Ontario, CA 91761-1567
1-800-388-4083

Biotech, Ltd.
18 N. State St.
Elgin, IL 60123-5414
1-800-525-2158

C.H.S. International, Inc.
550 39th Ave. N.E., #185
Columbia Heights, MN 55421
1-800-878-4550

Cascade Designs, Inc.
4000 1st Ave. S.
Seattle, WA 98134-2301
1-800-827-4548

Central Mattress Co.
501 N. 13th St.
Omaha, NE 68102
1-800-333-5376

Chestnut Ridge Foam, Inc.
P.O. Box 781
Latrobe, PA 15650-0781
1-800-234-2734

Chi`am International
P.O. Box 445
Circle Pines, MN 55014-0445
1-612-426-9046

Contour Fabricators, Inc.
4100 E. Baldwin Rd.
Grand Bianc, MI 48439
1-810-695-2910

Creative Bedding
Technologies, Inc.
18 N. State St.
Elgin, IL 60123-5414
1-800-526-2158

Crown Products Corp.
309 N. 17th St.
St. Louis, MO 63103-1708
1-800-779-3332

Danmar Products, Inc.
221 Jackson Industrial Dr.
Ann Arbor, MI 48103-9104
1-800-783-1998

Deroyal Industries, Inc.
200 Debusk Ln.
Powell, TN 37849-4703
1-800-251-9864

Dielectrics Medistad Corp.
270 Burnett Rd.
Chicopee, MA 01020-4636
1-800-345-4081

DNS Medical Supply, Inc./
Donsco Mfg., Inc.
4301 S. Valley View Blvd., #2
Las Vegas, NV 89103
1-800-553-5435

Ferguson Medical
3407 Bay Ave.
Chico, CA 95926-8619
1-916-342-4133

Flexi-Mat Corp.
2244 S. Western Ave.
Chicago, IL 60608-3893
1-800-338-7392

Floatation Systems, Inc.
P.O. Box 5070
Syracuse, NY 13220-5070
1-800-888-8529

Foam Cutting Engineers, Inc.
1235 National Ave.
Addison, IL 60101-3130
1-708-543-2855

Foam Products, Inc.
4747 Bronx Blvd.
Bronx, NY 10470-1001
1-800-283-4362

Foamex International, Inc.
1550 Champagne Ave.
Ontario, CA 91761
1-800-621-4163

Foxzy Products Corp.
9423 Enterprise Dr.
Mokena, IL 60448
1-708-479-3308

Freedom Designs, Inc.
2241 Madera Rd.
Simi Valley, CA 93065
1-800-331-8551

Geligne Medical
2150 Liberty Dr.
Niagara Falls, NY 14304
1-716-283-0700

Geriatric Products, Inc.
72 Division Pl.
Brooklyn, NY 11222-5230
1-800-435-3636

Geritrix Corp.
2 E. Sanford Blvd.
Mount Vernon, NY 10550
1-800-736-3437

Goldsouth Medical
2136 Stagecoach Rd.
Stockton, CA 95205-9001
1-800-366-0221

Graham-Field Aquatherm
400 Rabro Dr. E.
Hauppauge, NY 11788
1-800-645-8176

Grant Airmass Corp.
986 Bedford St.
Stamford, CT 06905-5610
1-800-243-5237

Healthcall Corp.
728 N. 7th St.
Milwaukee, WI 53233
1-800-558-7130

Hermell Products, Inc.
522 Cottage Grove Rd., Bldg. G
Bloomfield, CT 06002-3616
1-800-233-2342

Huntleigh Healthcare
227 Rte. 33 E.
Manalapan, NJ 07726-4238
1-800-223-1218

Ideal Medical Services Co.
9203 Zake Rd.
Houston, TX 77064
1-800-336-8020

Invacare Corp.
809 Cleveland St.
Elyria, OH 44036-2125
1-800-333-6900

J.J.Balan, Inc.
5725 Foster Ave.
Brooklyn, NY 11234-1001
1-800-552-2526

Jay Medical, LTD
4745 Walnut
Boulder, CO 80308
1-800-648-8282

Jefferson Industries, Inc.
1940 Rutgers University Blvd.
Lakewood, NJ 08701
1-800-257-5145

Kees Goebel Medical
Specialties, Inc.
9663 Glades Dr.
Hamilton, OH 45011-9402
1-800-354-0445

Ken McRight Supplies Inc.
7456 S. Oswego
Tulsa, OK 74136-5903
1-918-492-9657

Kendall-Futuro Co.
5405 Dupont Circle, Suite A
Milford, OH 45150
1-513-576-8000

Lotus Healthcare Products
31 Sheridan Dr.
Naugatuck, CT 06770-2034
1-800-243-2362

Lumex
81 Spence St.
Bay Shore, NY 11706-2231
1-800-645-5272

Madison Polymeric Engineering
495 Ward St. Extension
Wallingford, CT 06492
1-203-265-9550

Mastex Industries, Inc.
2035 Factory Ln.
Petersburg, VA 23803
1-800-343-7444

Med Group, Inc.
3223 S. Loop 289, Suite 600
Lubbock, TX 79423-1331
1-800-825-5633

Quickie Designs, Inc.
2842 Business Park Ave.
Fresno, CA 93727-1328
1-800-456-8168

Medifloat, Inc.
123 Orchard St., Suite 1 A/B
Ormond Beach, FL 32174
1-800-678-9299

Medpro, Inc.
1940 Rutgers University Blvd.
Lakewood, NJ 08701
1-800-257-5145

Mississippi Gulf South
Medical Supply
2136 Stagecoach Rd.
Stockton, CA 95215-7936
1-800-366-0221

MRC Industries, Inc., Mason
Medical Products
8000 Cooper Ave., Bldg. 28
Glendale, NY 11385-7734
1-800-233-4454

National Medical Products
6349 Beach Blvd.
Jacksonville, FL 32216-2707
1-800-940-6262

Pam Inc.
915 Carters Creek Pike
Columbia, TN 38401
1-800-214-6523

Perfect Rubber Seat Cushion Co.
6451 Edmund St.
Philadelphia, PA 19135-3313
1-215-333-3523

Posey Co., J.T.
5635 Peck Rd.
Arcadia, CA 91006-5851
1-800-447-6739

Production Research Corp.
10225 Southard Dr.
Beltsville, MD 20705-2193
1-800-772-1173

Profex Medical Products
P.O. Box 16043
St. Louis, MO 63105-3717
1-800-325-0196

Progressive Medical
Technology, Inc.
815 Terminal Rd.
Lansing, MI 48906-3062
1-800-572-0836

Quickie Designs, Inc.
2842 Business Park Ave.
Fresno, CA 93727-1328
1-800-456-8168

Regency Product International
1260 S. Boyle Ave.
Los Angeles, CA 90023-2602
1-800-845-7931

Roho, Inc.
100 Florida Ave.
Belleville, IL 62222-5429
1-800-850-7646

Safe-Guard Technologies Corp.
1111 Hector St.
Conshohocken, PA 19428-2311
1-800-220-1245

Sammons-Preston, Inc.
4 Sammons Ct.
Brook, IL 60440-5071
1-800-323-5547

Savant Medical
1215 S. Harlem
Forest Park, IL 60130-2407
1-708-771-2000

Schulman, Inc., DA
7701 Newton Ave. N.
Brooklyn Park, MN 55444-1911
1-612-561-2908

Sheepskin Ranch, Inc.
3115 Lackland Rd.
Fort Worth, TX 76116-4123
1-800-366-9950

Silipos
2150 Liberty Dr.
Niagara Falls, NY 14304
1-800-229-4404

Skil-Care Corp.
167 Saw Mill River Rd.
Yonkers, NY 10701-6605
1-800-431-2972

Smith & Nephew Rolyan, Inc.
N104 W13400 Donges Bay Rd.
Germantown, WI 53022
1-800-558-8633

Southwest Technologies, Inc.
2018 Baltimore
Kansas City, MO 64108-1914
1-800-247-9951

Span-American Medical
Systems, Inc.
P.O. Box 5231
Greenville, SC 29606-5231
1-800-888-6752

Spenco Medical Corp.
P.O. Box 2501
Waco, TX 76702-2501
1-800-877-3626

Steridyne Corp.
3725 Investment Ln.
Riviera Beach, FL 33404-1794
1-800-327-6185

Sunrise Medical
4083 E. Airport Dr.
Ontario, CA 91761
1-800-388-4083

Tex-Tenn Corp.
118 Kwickway
Gray, TN 37615
1-800-251-3027

Thompson Medical Specialties
4301 Bryant Ave. S.
Minneapolis, MN 55409-1708
1-800-777-4949

UFP Technologies, Inc.
172 E. Main St.
Georgetown, MA 01833-2107
1-508-352-2200

Vantage Industries, Inc.
4530-F Patton Dr. E.
Atlanta, GA 30336
1-800-221-4329

Ventura Enterprises
35 Lawton Ave.
Danville, IN 46122-1217
1-317-745-2989

Index